The Super Bowl's
Most Wanted™

Other football titles from Brassey's, Inc.

Big Play: Barra on Football, Allen Barra

Pro Football Forecast: 2004 Edition,
Sean Lahman and Todd Greanier

*Coaching Matters: Leadership and Tactics of the
NFL's Ten Greatest Coaches,* Brad Adler

*Dominance: The Best Seasons of Pro Football's
Greatest Teams,* Eddie Epstein

*Playing Hurt: Evaluating and Treating the
Warriors of the NFL,* Dr. Pierce E. Scranton

*Football's Most Wanted: The Top 10 Book of the
Great Game's Outrageous Characters, Fortunate
Fumbles, and Other Oddities,* Floyd Conner

The Super Bowl's Most Wanted™

The Top 10 Book of Big-Game Heroes, Pigskin Zeroes, and Championship Oddities

Walter Harvey

Brassey's, Inc.

WASHINGTON, D.C.

Library of Congress Cataloging-in-Publication Data

Harvey, Walter, 1967–
    The Super Bowl's most wanted : the top 10 book of
big-game heroes, pigskin zeroes, and championship oddities / Walter Harvey.-1st ed.
        p. cm.
    Includes bibliographical references and index.
    ISBN 1-57488-889-7 (pbk. : alk. paper)
    1. Super Bowl-History-Miscellanea. I. Title.

GV956.2.S8H37 2004
796.332'648-dc22   2004018488

Printed in Canada on acid-free paper that meets
the American National Standards Institute Z39-48
Standard.

Brassey's, Inc.
22841 Quicksilver Drive
Dulles, Virginia 20166

First Edition

10   9   8   7   6   5   4   3   2   1

Contents

List of Photographs

Acknowledgments

Special thanks go to my parents, Eileen and Walter. My mom instilled in me my love of books, and my dad gave me my love for football. Here's an example of how far back my dad and I go with football. When I was a five-year-old, my mother volunteered to be part of my church's Christmas party for the parish's kids. The party was held the Saturday before Christmas, December 23, 1972. What did I do? I told my mother I was staying home to watch football with my dad. Yup, I gave up Santa Claus, candy, and prizes to watch a game. What did I get for staying home? I got to see the "Immaculate Reception." It was at that moment that football had me for life.

Major thanks go out to Jim Cypher, my literary agent, who took a shot on an unproven author. Kevin Cuddihy and Chris Kahrl at Brassey's helped shape the book. Their efforts are greatly appreciated.

To my e-mail chain gang: Our sports discussions are always illuminating. Let's hope we're never Lemboed.

Lastly, I'd like to thank my wife, Larissa, without whose support this book would never have happened; and to my children, Megan and Joseph, I hope I get to celebrate a Jets' Super Bowl championship with you someday.

Introduction

In just four short decades, Super Bowl Sunday has grown from a hastily put together championship game to the biggest sports and entertainment spectacle in America.

The Super Bowl transcends football. Major cities now battle over the right to host the game—and to think, before Super Bowl I, the Rose Bowl turned down the opportunity to host. The game is always the highest-rated television program of the year, and a good percentage of the audience is watching for the commercials. And at two million dollars for thirty seconds of airtime, the commercial contest is as fierce as the game. The pregame and halftime shows now attract the biggest musical acts. U2, Beyoncé, Britney Spears, Bon Jovi, Aerosmith, just to name a few, have performed on Super Sunday. And, hey, don't forget to stay tuned after the game! The network will be showcasing a big show for the large audience lead-in.

But the real focus is, and always will be, the game itself. This book will celebrate the players, teams, and events that have helped shape the Super Bowl into a virtual national holiday. From the exploits of veteran carouser Max McGee in Super Bowl I through the last-second heroics of Adam Vinatieri in Super Bowl XXXVIII, *The Super Bowl's Most Wanted* covers it all.

The Vince Lombardi Trophy is something to be cherished. Lombardi's Packers won the first two Super Bowls. They didn't get another trophy for twenty-nine years. The Pittsburgh Steelers went forty years without winning a championship; then they won four in six years. Now they've gone another twenty-four years without one. The Jets won Super Bowl III but haven't been back since. The Dolphins won the Super Bowl in just their seventh season of existence. They repeated their victory the following year, but have gone more than three decades now without winning again.

And it isn't just teams who cherish the trophy. John Elway had done everything through the first fifteen years of his illustrious career, but he'd lost the only three Super Bowls he competed in. And he also held the Super Bowl record for career interceptions thrown. But in Super Bowl XXXII, at the age of 37, he got his first Super Bowl championship. He liked it so much he came back the next year to win another one and then hung up his cleats. Dan Marino of the Dolphins, drafted the same year as Elway, reached the big game in his record-breaking season of 1984, his second in the league. After losing to the 49ers, Marino thought he'd be back a number of times, but he retired after the 1999 season without ever having returned.

If you're a fan, the great moments are etched in your mind: Joe Montana's last-minute heroics in Super Bowl XXIII; Marcus Allen's long run; Lynn Swann's fantastic catches in Super Bowl X; Ricky Proehl's game-tying touchdown grabs in two Super Bowls, only to see his team foiled by Adam Vinatieri on the games' final plays; Kurt Warner's fantastic performance in Super Bowl XXXIV. In these pages you can relive these and other lesser-known events. Ever hear of Skipper McNally? Don McCafferty? Tim Smith? Brent McClanahan (no, he wasn't a star on *The Golden Girls*)? You'll know their names after reading their stories here.

So get yourself taped up, and buckle up for a journey through thirty-eight years of Super Bowl magic.

Somebody
Had to Do It

Before there was Brett Favre, there was Bart Starr. Before Jack Squirek, Herb Adderley. Before Muhsin Muhammad, Max McGee. Here are the famous firsts in Super Bowl history.

1. FIRST TOUCHDOWN

It won't be remembered by Bart Starr as one of his prettiest throws. But in the first quarter of Super Bowl I, facing a third-down-and-three, the Green Bay quarterback found reserve wide receiver Max McGee on a slant pattern, isolated on Kansas City's Fred Williamson. The pass was behind McGee, who caught it with one hand at the 23-yard line, then galloped into the end zone with Williamson trailing to score the first points in Super Bowl history.

2. FIRST INTERCEPTION RETURN FOR A TOUCHDOWN

The Green Bay Packers were shutting the door on Super Bowl II, leading the Oakland Raiders, 26–7, in the fourth quarter when future Hall of Famer Herb

Adderley slammed the door on the Raiders. Adderley stepped in front of Fred Biletnikoff, who didn't seem ready for the pass, and scooted 60 yards for the touchdown and the last points for the Packers in their 33–14 win.

3. FIRST GAME ON ARTIFICIAL TURF

Need a sign to indicate that artificial turf is a really bad thing? Super Bowl V, the turnover-filled snooze fest between the Colts and the Cowboys at Miami's Orange Bowl, was the first Super Bowl played on carpet. Four of the next five were held on turf as well. Interestingly, the Orange Bowl hosted two games on grass, then two more on turf, and finally went back to grass for Super Bowl XIII. One other site, Tulane Stadium, also hosted games on both the real stuff and the carpet.

4. FIRST PENALTY

Super Bowl I was strange in so many ways that we can't even award an individual with the dubious honor of first Super Bowl penalty. That distinction goes to the Kansas City Chiefs team, who was whistled for a delay of game infraction in their first series.

5. FIRST TEAM NOT TO SCORE A TOUCHDOWN

When people think of the Miami Dolphins of the 1970s, they immediately think of the perfect season of 1972, or the two consecutive Super Bowl championships. They generally don't bring up Miami's futility in Super Bowl VI against the Cowboys, when they became the first team not to score a touchdown in a Super Bowl game. Their three points, in fact, is still a record for futility. Other than one field goal, the Dolphins threatened to reach the end zone only once. Trailing 24–3 in the fourth quarter, they advanced to the Dallas 16-yard line before Bob Griese turned the ball over with a fumble.

6. FIRST MISSED EXTRA POINT

He gets a lot of glory for beating Dallas in Super Bowl V with a field goal in the final seconds. But Baltimore's Jim O'Brien may not have been in a situation to attempt the game-winning kick had he not had an earlier point-after-touchdown attempt blocked.

7. FIRST SAFETY

It's appropriate that the Steel Curtain, one of the most dominant defenses in NFL history, was responsible for the Super Bowl's first safety. Super Bowl IX was scoreless, and the Minnesota Vikings had the ball at their own 9-yard line in the second quarter. Vikings quarterback Fran Tarkenton botched a handoff attempt and the ball rolled back toward the goal line. Tarkenton alertly fell on the ball about a yard into the end zone, where he was downed by Steelers defensive tackle Dwight White.

8. FIRST FUMBLE RETURN FOR A TOUCHDOWN

Back to those Dolphins again. For a team as great as they were, they find themselves on this list twice. In Super Bowl VII Garo Yepremian's folly on a blocked field goal turned into the first fumble recovery for a touchdown in Super Bowl history, as Washington Redskins defensive back Mike Bass rumbled 49 yards for a score to cut a seemingly insurmountable four-teen-point deficit down to a touchdown.

9. FIRST KICKOFF RETURN FOR A TOUCHDOWN

Finally, we can say something positive about Miami. It was Fulton Walker, a backup defensive back for the

Dolphins, who scored on a kickoff return in Super Bowl XVII against the Redskins. That score gave the Dolphins a lead they held onto until the fourth quarter, when John Riggins rumbled for 43 yards and the go-ahead touchdown.

10. FIRST PUNT RETURN FOR A TOUCHDOWN

Trick! Through the first thirty-eight Super Bowls, there have been no touchdowns scored on punt returns.

The Buck Stops Here

There's an old saying in sports that defense wins championships. This has never been truer than in the Super Bowl, where the top defensive teams almost always come out on top. Below are the top ten defensive units to take the field on Super Bowl Sunday.

1. CHICAGO BEARS, SUPER BOWL XX

On the second play from scrimmage of Super Bowl XX, the New England Patriots recovered a fumble by Chicago Bears running back Walter Payton on the Chicago 19-yard line. For the next three plays, New England gained zero yards and settled for a field goal. How many more times did the Patriots get into Bears' territory the rest of the game? Twice. The Bears' defense, led by Super Bowl MVP Richard Dent, was overwhelming. The Patriots managed only 7 net yards rushing; starting quarterback Tony Eason was zero for six passing; and the Bears forced six turnovers in a 46–10 wipeout.

2. BALTIMORE RAVENS, SUPER BOWL XXXV

The Baltimore Ravens set a record in 2000, allowing the fewest total points in sixteen games, and Super Bowl XXXV against the New York Giants was a super culmination to their magnificent season. The Giants were able to muster only 152 total yards, and the Ravens, led by MVP Ray Lewis, forced five turnovers and recorded four sacks. The biggest play in the game was recorded by cornerback Duane Starks in the third quarter, when he stepped in front of Giants receiver Amani Toomer, picked off Kerry Collins's pass, and returned it 49 yards for a touchdown that gave Baltimore a 17–0 lead. The final score was 34–7, and the Giants' only points came on a Ron Dixon kickoff return for a touchdown.

3. PITTSBURGH STEELERS, SUPER BOWL IX

Pittsburgh's Steel Curtain was one of the greatest defensive units ever assembled, but they were never more dominant in a big spot than in their first championship, a 16–6 win in Super Bowl IX over the Minnesota Vikings. On a cold, damp afternoon at Tulane Stadium in New Orleans, Pittsburgh's defense absolutely put a stranglehold on the Minnesota offense, holding quarterback Fran Tarkenton to eleven completions in twenty-six attempts for a mere 102 yards passing, and controlling the Vikings' ground attack to just 17 yards rushing. In addition, Dwight White produced the first safety in Super Bowl history, dropping Tarkenton in the end zone in the second quarter. For the game, the Steelers forced five Minnesota turnovers.

4. TAMPA BAY BUCCANEERS, SUPER BOWL XXXVII

The Tampa Bay Buccaneers came into Super Bowl XXXVII against the Oakland Raiders with one of the top defenses in the NFL. But the Raiders had what was widely considered the best offensive unit in the league, led by NFL MVP Rich Gannon and future Hall of Fame wide receivers Jerry Rice and Tim Brown. But the Bucs jumped to an early lead, thanks to Super Bowl MVP Dexter Jackson's two interceptions, and the Raiders never recovered. In the second half, when the Raiders tried to mount a comeback, the Bucs' defense got into the scoring act, returning three interceptions for touchdowns, including two by Dwight Smith and one by 2002 NFL Defensive Player of the Year Derrick Brooks to cap off their 48–21 victory. The Raiders managed to make the score somewhat respectable only after the Bucs had taken a thirty-one-point third quarter lead.

5. DALLAS COWBOYS, SUPER BOWL XII

The Dallas Cowboys entered Super Bowl XII against the Denver Broncos on a roll. They went 12–2 during the regular season, and then buried the Bears and the Vikings in the playoffs by a combined 60–13 score. Some were calling this Tom Landry's best team in Dallas, and his defense proved the point at the Superdome. Co-MVPs Randy White and Harvey Martin led a ferocious pass rush that tormented Denver quarterback Craig Morton, who completed only four of fifteen passes before being replaced by Norris Weese. In their 27–10 win the Cowboys intercepted four passes and recovered four Denver fumbles to set a Super Bowl record for takeaways.

6. LOS ANGELES RAIDERS, SUPER BOWL XVIII

As Super Bowl XVIII approached, many people knew the Los Angeles Raiders were a good football team with a talented defense, led by stars like Howie Long,

Lyle Alzado, Ted Hendricks, Lester Hayes, and Mike Haynes. But the Redskins? The defending Super Bowl champs boasted one of the best offenses in history, setting an NFL record with 541 points in the regular season (a staggering average of 33.8 points per game). But against the Raiders, their offense could generate nothing. Running back John Riggins, who had devoured the Dolphins in the previous Super Bowl, could manage only 64 yards rushing on twenty-six carries, and Joe Theismann, continually frustrated by the tight man coverage by cornerbacks Hayes and Haynes, was able to complete only sixteen out of thirty-five passes, with two picks, the biggest coming late in the second quarter, when Jack Squirek intercepted a swing pass and returned it 5 yards for a touchdown that gave the Raiders a 21–3 lead, effectively closing the game out.

7. NEW ENGLAND PATRIOTS, SUPER BOWL XXXVI

When you look at the New England Patriots' total defensive stats, they aren't all that impressive. However, the Pats pushed around a well-balanced St. Louis Rams attack, holding them to only one field goal through the first three quarters. Marshall Faulk, the Rams' MVP running back, gained only 76 yards against the stingy New England front seven. They wilted somewhat in the fourth quarter, but they still held the greatest show on turf to just seventeen points. Kurt Warner threw for 365 yards, but he was picked off twice, the first time by cornerback Ty Law, who returned it 47 yards for the Patriots' first touchdown.

8. WASHINGTON REDSKINS, SUPER BOWL XVII

The Washington Redskins of the early 1980s are best remembered for their Fun Bunch offense, but they had a solid defense spearheaded by defensive linemen Dave Butz and Dexter Manley. In Super Bowl XVII against the Miami Dolphins, the Redskins defense had just one major hiccup—a 76-yard first-quarter touchdown pass from David Woodley to Jimmy Cefalo. The rest of the afternoon, they were near perfect, allowing the Dolphins only 176 yards total offense and just three other completed passes for the remainder of the game. They also forced two turnovers—a Butz recovery of a Woodley fumble following a sack by Manley, and an interception by safety Mark Murphy.

9. MIAMI DOLPHINS, SUPER BOWL VII

When the Miami Dolphins and the Washington Redskins first met in the Super Bowl, the outcome was much different. The Dolphins completed their perfect season in a flawless 14–7 win at the L.A. Coliseum. The Redskins managed just sixteen first downs and only 228 total yards. Manny Fernandez led the charge, stifling the Washington running attack, and the Dolphins also picked off three Billy Kilmer passes, two by MVP Jake Scott and a third by Nick Buoniconti that set up Miami's second touchdown.

10. DALLAS COWBOYS, SUPER BOWL VI

No team has scored fewer points in a Super Bowl game than Miami's three in Super Bowl VI against the Dallas Cowboys. Against a veteran Dallas defense that included Bob Lilly, Jethro Pugh, Lee Roy Jordan, Herb Adderley, and Mel Renfro, the Dolphins managed to march into Cowboys' territory only five times. Bob Griese was hurried in the pocket all game and managed to complete only twelve passes. The Dolphins managed only 185 net yards. Dallas linebacker Chuck Howley followed up an MVP performance in Super

Bowl V by intercepting a pass and recovering a fumble. Both of his takeaways led to Dallas touchdowns as the Cowboys cruised to their first-ever world championship, 24–3.

not in My House

Above are the top team defensive performances in the Super Bowl. Here are the top individual defensive performances.

1. RAY LEWIS

In Super Bowl XXXV the Ravens' Ray Lewis did not have a single interception or sack, but the New York Giants did not run a single play without thinking of where Lewis would be. He had four passes defensed, including one that led to an interception, and five tackles. But his presence alone altered the New York offense.

2. RICHARD DENT

Richard Dent made his presence felt early on the New England offense in Super Bowl XX. Dent forced two fumbles among his four first-half tackles. He also batted down one pass and recorded one and a half sacks. Although the entire Chicago defensive unit was good, Dent was just the best.

3. MANNY FERNANDEZ

As the anchor of the Miami Dolphins' line, tackle Manny Fernandez was their best defensive player in their three straight Super Bowls in the early 1970s. But his best performance came in Super Bowl VII, with Miami's perfect season on the line. Fernandez recorded six tackles, two of those for losses, and also had a sack of Billy Kilmer, as the Dolphins held the Redskins without an offensive touchdown in their 14–7 win. Safety Jake Scott, who had two interceptions, was named the game's MVP, but Fernandez easily could have argued for a share.

4. MEAN JOE GREENE

On those great Pittsburgh Steelers teams of the 1970s, it's hard to single out one individual for his defensive efforts. But in Super Bowl IX against the Vikings, Joe Greene gets special attention for helping to completely shut down the Minnesota rushing game. At the same time he hounded Fran Tarkenton into a miserable performance. Then, in the fourth quarter with the Steelers trying to hold on for their first-ever championship, Greene recorded an interception and recovered a fumble to thwart Vikings' drives.

5, 6. LESTER HAYES AND MIKE HAYNES

Lester Hayes and Mike Haynes were shutdown corners on the Raiders' Super Bowl XVIII championship team. It was their coverage on the Washington Redskins' wide receivers that frustrated quarterback Joe Theismann all afternoon. Theismann completed just five passes to wide receivers all game, despite the offensive records his team set during the regular season. Haynes also had one of the Raiders' two interceptions.

7. HACKSAW REYNOLDS

Super Bowl XVI saw Jack "Hacksaw" Reynolds in his second Super Bowl in three years, having played for the Rams in their Super Bowl XIV loss to the Steelers. With the 49ers this time, he was determined not to lose again. Against the Bengals, Reynolds had eight tackles and a sack out of his middle linebacker position. But no defensive plays were more important than his two stops on bruising running back Pete Johnson during a third-quarter goal-line stand. Reynolds stopped him for no gain on a second-down play from the 1-yard line, then on fourth down, Reynolds stopped Johnson for no gain again. The defensive stand kept the score 20–7 in favor of the 49ers, and they eventually held on to win the game, 26–21.

8. HARVEY MARTIN

Dallas defensive end Harvey Martin was co-MVP of Super Bowl XII with his line mate, Randy White. The Denver Broncos' quarterbacks, former Cowboy Craig Morton and Norris Weese, won't forget Martin applying pressure on seemingly every down.

9. DWIGHT SMITH

In Super Bowl XXXVII Tampa Bay cornerback Dwight Smith became the first player in Super Bowl history to return two interceptions for touchdowns. Smith's first pick came in the third quarter, when he stepped in front of Jerry Rice and raced down the sideline. That extended the Tampa Bay lead over the Oakland Raiders to 34–3. Then in the closing moments, he picked off Rich Gannon a second time, returning it 50 yards for the final points of a 48–21 victory. Despite the record, Smith's secondary mate, Dexter Jackson,

whose two first-half interceptions helped the Buccaneers build their big lead, was named MVP.

10.   CHUCK HOWLEY

A linebacker for the Cowboys, Chuck Howley is the
only player from a losing team to win the Super Bowl
MVP award, a feat he accomplished in Dallas's Super
Bowl V loss to the Baltimore Colts. But Howley had a
big game the following year as well. In Super Bowl VI
Howley had a fumble recovery and another intercep-
tion. Both takeaways led to Dallas scores as the
Cowboys stormed over the Dolphins, 24–3.

I Left My Heart in . . .

L ocation, location, location. Anyone wanting to buy or sell a home has heard that phrase a few times. And if your city wants to host a Super Bowl, location is important—really important. That's because the NFL wants to ensure mild temperatures for the game, and Super Bowls are awarded only to warm-weather cities or cities with domes. The most common host cities follow.

1. **MIAMI, FLORIDA**

Miami has played host to eight Super Bowls, five at the Orange Bowl and three at Pro Player Stadium. From the historic—Lombardi's final game with the Packers in Super Bowl II, the Jets' stunning upset of the Colts in Super Bowl III, and Super Bowl XXIII's remarkable comeback by the 49ers—to the spectacular—O'Brien's winning field goal in Super Bowl V and Lynn Swann's acrobatics in Super Bowl X versus the Cowboys—Miami has seen just about everything. Just don't invite Dallas. The Cowboys' franchise has gone

5–3 in their eight Super Bowl appearances, and all three of their losses occurred in the Orange Bowl.

2. NEW ORLEANS, LOUISIANA

Pre–Super Bowl parties are always memorable on Bourbon Street, but the games often leave a lot to be desired. You could call New Orleans "blowout central." The average score in games played there is 30–10. Tulane Stadium, a rickety old dump that played host to three games, probably gets the nod for the Super Bowl game played in the worst weather, Super Bowl IX, a damp, dreary affair won by the Steelers over the Vikings. The most uncompetitive Super Bowl ever, San Francisco's 55–10 dismantling of Denver in Super Bowl XXIV, was played there, in the Superdome. But with New England's 20–17 win over St. Louis in Super Bowl XXXVI, New Orleans also can lay claim to hosting one of the greatest Super Bowls ever played.

Toby Valadie/Louisiana Superdome

The Louisiana Superdome in New Orleans
gets set to host Super Bowl XXXVI.

3. PASADENA, CALIFORNIA

The Rose Bowl may be the most beautiful setting for a Super Bowl game. In fact, Pete Rozelle had hoped to play Super Bowl I there, but he met resistance from the Tournament of Roses committee, so the game was played in Los Angeles. More than 100,000 fans fill the ageless oval, which looks like it's in better shape than many newer stadiums. Pasadena has hosted five Super Bowl games, the most memorable, believe it or not, was a blowout, the Cowboys' Super Bowl XXVII romp over the Bills. The Rose Bowl also holds distinction as the last Super Bowl in which it was still daylight when the final gun sounded—Super Bowl XI.

4. TAMPA, FLORIDA

The site of three Super Bowls, Tampa will remain in the rotation of Super Bowl host cities for years to come, thanks to its gorgeous weather and the sleek Raymond James Stadium. Two of Tampa's Super Bowl games have been blowouts where defense dominated, Super Bowl XVIII, when the Raiders thumped the Redskins, and Super Bowl XXXV, in which the Ravens overwhelmed the Giants. The other game? Probably the best Super Bowl ever played, the New York Giants' thrilling 20–19 win over the Buffalo Bills in Super Bowl XXV.

5. SAN DIEGO, CALIFORNIA

Beautiful weather has been the backdrop to the three Super Bowls played at Jack Murphy/Qualcomm Stadium. Each of the games has had some historical significance: Super Bowl XXII had the first African-American quarterback to win the game, as Doug Williams led the Redskins over the Broncos, 42–10;

Super Bowl XXXII saw John Elway finally win a Super Bowl for the Broncos, 31–24 over the defending champion Packers, in a game that was also the first AFC win over the NFC in fourteen years; and Super Bowl XXXVII was the first in which a coach faced a team he had coached the previous year, as Jon Gruden led his Tampa Bay Buccaneers to a 48–21 win over the Oakland Raiders, with whom he had been for four years.

6. LOS ANGELES, CALIFORNIA

The Los Angeles Rams had called the L.A. Coliseum home from 1946 through 1979 and had employed future NFL Commissioner Pete Rozelle in their front office. While Rozelle was there, the Coliseum routinely drew crowds of 85,000-plus, so it seemed natural to put the first-ever Super Bowl in such a huge venue. But Super Bowl I, featuring the Green Bay Packers and Kansas City Chiefs, was played to more than 30,000 empty seats. Fortunately for the NFL, that was the last Super Bowl not to sell every ticket. The Super Bowl returned to Los Angeles on one other occasion, Super Bowl VII, as the Miami Dolphins finished off a perfect 17–0 season with a 14–7 win over the Washington Redskins.

7. ATLANTA, GEORGIA

It's never good when people remember the Super Bowl host city for events that happen off the field and not on it. Such is the case with Atlanta. Super Bowl XXVIII, the first of two Atlanta Super Bowls, passed without incident, as the Cowboys defeated the Bills, 30–13, for their second straight championship. But Super Bowl XXXIV was almost doomed from the start. A cold front and ice storm blanketed the area, and the city was ill prepared for the conditions. There were no salt trucks for the streets, which made driving an exercise in street luge. Teams were forced to practice walk-throughs in hotel ballrooms, as the streets were unsafe for buses. The game turned out to be a classic, though, as the Rams edged the Tennessee Titans, 23–16.

When the game was over, a celebration at a night-club in the exclusive Buckhead neighborhood grew ugly, ending in the stabbing deaths of two men. The men responsible were traced back to a group that included Baltimore Ravens linebacker Ray Lewis. Lewis eventually stood trial for murder but was acquitted. Two men in Lewis's group were convicted in the deaths.

8. PONTIAC, MICHIGAN

One of only two cold-weather cities to host the Super Bowl (Minneapolis being the other), Pontiac, Michigan, the home of the Detroit Lions, was the first place that Super Bowl visitors had to worry about the wind chill factor. In fact, the day the Cincinnati Bengals arrived for the 1982 game against the 49ers, it was twelve degrees below zero, with snow, ice, and slush covering the streets. This weather pretty much ensured that Super Bowl XVI would be the only one ever played at the Silverdome, and the two teams made it a good one, with San Francisco prevailing, 26–21.

But, apparently, the NFL can't stay away from the Motor City. Detroit will host a future Super Bowl in their glitzy new downtown stadium, Ford Field.

9. PALO ALTO, CALIFORNIA

Stanford Stadium played host to Super Bowl XIX, a game that pitted the 14–2 Miami Dolphins against the

15–1 San Francisco 49ers. A virtual home game for the 49ers, they played like the home team, dismantling the Dolphins, 38–16, in the only Super Bowl played in northern California.

10. HOUSTON, TEXAS

Houston played host to a cool, misty, game in Super Bowl VIII, as the Miami Dolphins walloped the Minnesota Vikings, 24–7. "What?" you say. "Cool and misty at the old Astrodome? Impossible." Well, even though it was called the Eighth Wonder of the World and was the home of the AFC's Houston Oilers, the Astrodome was *not* the site of the game. The NFL deemed its capacity too small (it only held around 50,000), so Super Bowl VIII was played outdoors at Rice Stadium, the home of Rice University's Owls. The Super Bowl did not return to Houston until Super Bowl XXXVIII in January 2004, at the glitzy, convertible-dome Reliant Stadium—and this was one of the best Super Bowls ever played, as New England knocked off Carolina, 32–29.

Some Nice Parting Gifts

Joe Theismann has been quoted as saying he'd rather his team be eliminated before the Super Bowl than lose the Super Bowl. There are plenty of teams who felt the same way after being thoroughly beaten on Super Bowl Sunday. These are the teams who have suffered the most humiliating Super Bowl losses.

1. DENVER BRONCOS, SUPER BOWL XXIV

The San Francisco 49ers set eighteen Super Bowl records as they dismantled the Denver Broncos, 55–10. They led 13–3 after the first quarter and 27–3 at the half. The Broncos could muster only twelve first downs and 167 total yards of offense. The blowout was so bad that San Francisco offensive tackle Bubba Paris even said: "It got to a point where, being a Christian and being a person who loves people, I actually felt sorry for the Broncos."

Jon SooHoo

John Elway and the Broncos suffered the worst loss in Super
Bowl history, dropping Super Bowl XXIV 55–10 to the 49ers.

2. NEW ENGLAND PATRIOTS, SUPER BOWL XX

Heading into Super Bowl XX, the Chicago Bears were talked about as one of the best defensive teams of all time, and once the game started, the New England Patriots did nothing to change fans' minds. New England's only touchdown in their 46–10 loss came in the fourth quarter when they trailed by forty-one points and when most of the Bears' defensive starters were on the bench. They rushed for a whopping 7— that's right, 7—total yards. At least the Patriots could take solace in the fact that they were the only team to advance to a Super Bowl after winning three straight road games.

3. DENVER BRONCOS, SUPER BOWL XXII

Thirteen teams have surrendered more than thirty-five points in a Super Bowl game. But against the Washington Redskins in Super Bowl XXII, the Denver Broncos set a new record for futility by giving up thirty-five points in the *second quarter* alone on their way to a 42–10 loss. The Redskins ran eighteen plays in the second quarter, and they turned five of them into touchdowns. The Broncos were victimized by three of the best Super Bowl individual performances of all time: Redskins quarterback Doug Williams threw for 340 yards and four touchdowns; wide receiver Gary Sanders caught nine passes for 193 yards and two touchdowns; and rookie back Tim Smith rushed for a Super Bowl record 204 yards and two touchdowns.

4. OAKLAND RAIDERS, SUPER BOWL XXXVII

Despite having one of the most prolific offenses of all time, the Oakland Raiders could not muster any semblance of an offensive attack as they were defeated by the Tampa Bay Buccaneers, 48–21. Rich Gannon was intercepted five times (three of which were brought back for touchdowns), and the Raiders did not score their first touchdown until the third quarter, by which time they trailed 34–3.

5. WASHINGTON REDSKINS, SUPER BOWL XVIII

The Washington Redskins finished the 1983 season with a 14–2 record and entered the Super Bowl being hailed as one of the best teams of all time. But they could muster just 283 total yards as both Joe Theismann and John Riggins suffered subpar games, and the Raiders dominated all three phases of the game. When the Redskins scored their only touchdown in the third quarter to draw within twelve points of their opponents, the Raiders responded with a touchdown of their own, and the 38–9 rout was assured.

6. BUFFALO BILLS, SUPER BOWL XXVII

Most remember that the Cowboys destroyed the Buffalo Bills, 52–17, the first time they met in the Super Bowl. But few remember that the Bills scored the first touchdown of the game and that they were intercepted in the end zone early in the second quarter when they had a chance to tie. That's what happens when a Pro Bowl running back (Thurman Thomas) rushes for only 19 yards, and the team's offense turns the ball over nine times.

7. SAN DIEGO CHARGERS, SUPER BOWL XXIX

After seven offensive plays in Super Bowl XXIX, the 49ers had scored fourteen points, and the rout was on. The San Diego Chargers were never competitive, trailing 14–7 after one quarter, 28–10 at the half, and 42–18 at the end of three. San Francisco's Steve Young threw for 325 yards and six (six!) touchdowns. The Chargers also had no answer for Jerry Rice, who scorched their secondary for 149 yards receiving, or for Ricky Watters, who had 108 total yards. Oh, yeah. Rice and Watters also scored three touchdowns each in their 49–26 win.

8. MIAMI DOLPHINS, SUPER BOWL XIX

The Miami Dolphins had one of the best passing games in recent memory, led by second-year quarterback Dan Marino. In the first quarter of Super Bowl XIX, Marino completed nine of his first ten passes to help stake Miami to a 10–7 lead over the San Francisco 49ers. But that was just about all the offense the Dolphins could muster. The 49ers, who were 15–1 during the regular season, stormed to three consecutive second-quarter touchdowns, and never looked back. The Dolphins could not stop the 49ers' balanced offense all day, and on the offensive side of the ball, they rushed for just 25 yards in a 38–16 defeat.

9. MINNESOTA VIKINGS, SUPER BOWL IV

Super Bowl IV was supposed to be a blowout, but no one expected the Minnesota Vikings, a 12½-point favorite of the oddsmakers, to be on the short end of the final score against the Kansas City Chiefs. But Kansas City's solid defense kept the Vikings' offense in check all afternoon, surrendering only twelve first downs and a single touchdown in the third quarter in their 23–7 win. On the other side of the ball, the Chiefs rushed for 151 yards, and MVP Len Dawson completed twelve of seventeen passes for 146 yards and a touchdown. The Vikings became the second consecutive NFL champion to lose to the AFL champion in the Super Bowl.

10.   NEW YORK GIANTS, SUPER BOWL XXXV

The New York Giants went up against one of the best defenses of all time when they played the Baltimore Ravens in Super Bowl XXXV, and like most teams that faced the Ravens in 2000, they were roughed up, losing 34–7. The Giants had only eleven first downs (and three of those came on Baltimore penalties) and managed only 2.6 yards per offensive play. Giants quarterback Kerry Collins was harassed all day and tossed four interceptions. The Giants only avoided the indignity of a shutout on Ron Dixon's 97-yard kickoff return for a touchdown.

What If . . .

When you're a fan of the losing Super Bowl team, you spend days, weeks, sometimes years, wondering what might have been. It's easy enough to dismiss a one-sided loss, but the close ones really stick in your craw. Here are the big what-ifs in Super Bowl history.

1. BALTIMORE COLTS, SUPER BOWL III

Super Bowl III was rife with what-ifs for the Colts. Suppose Don Shula had brought in Johnny Unitas off the bench earlier? Suppose Earl Morrall had hit Jimmy Orr in the end zone on the final play of the first half? And what about their first possession? The Colts ran eleven plays and ate up close to 5½ minutes off the clock, but came away with no points when Lou Michaels missed a 27-yard field goal. Michaels also missed a 46-yarder in the second quarter. In a low-scoring game those wasted opportunities crippled Baltimore's chances.

2. DALLAS COWBOYS, SUPER BOWL V

Super Bowl V resembled a preseason Pop Warner game with all of its penalties and turnovers. But early in the third quarter, the Cowboys seemed to have all the momentum. They led 13–6, thanks to a goal-line stand at the end of the first half. Then they recovered a fumble on the second-half kickoff. Five straight runs put the ball on the Colts' 1-yard line. But Cowboys running back Duane Thomas coughed the ball up, and the Colts recovered. If Thomas had scored and Dallas had gone up 20–6, the Colts, playing as they had in the first half, likely would not have recovered from that deficit.

3. MINNESOTA VIKINGS, SUPER BOWL IX

The Vikings were awful in Super Bowl IX; their offense could get nothing going, and the Steelers decimated their defensive running game. But they trailed only 9–6 early in the fourth quarter, following a touchdown on a blocked punt. With the Steelers facing a third and two at their own 42-yard line, Pittsburgh quarterback Terry Bradshaw hit Larry Brown with a 30-yard pass down the right side. But Brown fumbled, and the Vikings recovered the ball with a chance to tie or take the lead! After officials talked it over, however, they ruled (correctly) that Brown was down by contact before he lost the ball. The Steelers went on to a game-clinching touchdown.

4. DALLAS COWBOYS, SUPER BOWL X

The Cowboys trailed the Steelers 15–10 with a little over three minutes left in Super Bowl X. On a third-and-four play for Pittsburgh, Terry Bradshaw was leveled by Dallas tackle Larry Cole on a pass play, knocking the quarterback unconscious. Bradshaw was through for the rest of the game, but incredibly, the pass he got off was completed to Lynn Swann for a 64-yard touchdown. The Steelers led 21–10 and eventually won 21–17. Cowboys fans could only wonder what could have happened if that pass had not been completed.

5. DALLAS COWBOYS, SUPER BOWL XIII

Ask Dallas fans about Super Bowl XIII, and they still get red in the face over a fourth-quarter pass interference penalty on Cowboys cornerback Bennie Barnes. With the Pittsburgh Steelers hanging on to a 21–17 lead, Barnes and Pittsburgh's Lynn Swann got their feet tangled on a deep pass to the right side of the field, and both hit the turf. The controversial flag went against Barnes, resulting in a 33-yard penalty. The play completely changed the momentum of the game, as Pittsburgh scored two touchdowns on the next four plays from scrimmage to ice the game.

6. BUFFALO BILLS, SUPER BOWL XXV

Bruce Smith did everything right in Super Bowl XXV. Buffalo's All-Pro defensive end beat his man and sacked Giants quarterback Jeff Hostetler for a safety, which gave the Bills a 12–3 second-quarter lead. But when Smith tried to strip Hostetler, grabbing at his right arm, the quarterback did a great job to hold on to the ball. Had Hostetler fumbled and the Bills recovered, Buffalo would have had a lead of two touchdowns. How significant would that lead have been? No team in Super Bowl history has ever recovered from a two-touchdown deficit to win the game.

7. BUFFALO BILLS, SUPER BOWL XXVIII

The Bills were desperate to snap their three-game Super Bowl losing streak with Super Bowl XXVIII. They led the Cowboys, who had embarrassed them just one year earlier, by a score of 10–6. They had the ball at the Dallas 12-yard line with twenty-seven seconds left in the half but went conservative, throwing three passes, none to the end zone. Settling for a Steve Christie field goal, they led the game 13–6, but a touchdown would have put them up by eleven and could have been a huge psychological boost for a team that had suffered so much heartache. As it turned out, those were the last points the Bills scored in the game, which they lost, 30–13.

8. NEW ENGLAND PATRIOTS, SUPER BOWL XXXI

Just kick it somewhere else! That's what Patriots' fans had to think at the end of Super Bowl XXXI, after Green Bay's Desmond Howard won the game's MVP award with 244 all-purpose return yards. The pivotal play in the game was Howard's 99-yard kickoff return for a touchdown immediately following a New England touchdown that had brought the Patriots within 27–21. Howard's return was the final score in the game, and folks all over New England wished they could have that one kickoff back.

9. GREEN BAY PACKERS, SUPER BOWL XXXII

Could the Packers defense have held the Broncos at the 1-yard line with two minutes left in Super Bowl XXXII? We'll never know. The Packers had no timeouts left and opted to let the Broncos score a touchdown in order to get the ball back. Otherwise, the Broncos could have run the clock all the way down and kicked a field goal at the gun. The strategy seemed logical at the time, but how about forcing a turnover or blocking the kick? Or even better, why not stop the Broncos from getting down the field so easily?

10. OAKLAND RAIDERS, SUPER BOWL XXXVII

If you're going into the biggest game of the year and the opposing team is coached by the same man who just a year earlier was your own coach, you'll be sure to change up play calls and formations, no? Well, apparently not if you're the Oakland Raiders, who headed to Super Bowl XXXVII in January 2003. Jon Gruden's Buccaneers defense was calling out the Raiders' plays right as they were lining up. So it is easy to explain how Tampa Bay intercepted Rich Gannon five times, returning three of them for touchdowns.

No, You Take It

Isn't the Super Bowl supposed to be the showcase game of the season, featuring the two best teams? Then why is it that so many teams play like the ball is a Mexican jumping bean? Remarkably, turnovers have told the tale of many Super Bowls.

1. SUPER BOWL V

If a cautionary video on the dangers of turning the ball over is ever created, Super Bowl V should be a focal point. Dallas and Baltimore combined for eleven turnovers. Talk about getting tight in the big game. But how about the Dallas second half? Running back Duane Thomas's fumble on the 1-yard line on the Cowboys' first possession started it. Quarterback Craig Morton's three fourth-quarter interceptions (which led to ten Colts points) ended it.

2. SUPER BOWL III

In Super Bowl III, the Jets played a great game, and when you get right down to it, the Colts played a sloppy game. But the play that signaled the end for the Colts came on the last play of the first half. New York safety Jim Hudson's interception (one of five Colts' turnovers) of Baltimore quarterback Earl Morrall came on a flea-flicker play, a play on which Morrall missed a wide-open Jimmy Orr in the end zone.

3. SUPER BOWL XI

This was going to be the Vikings' year! Everything was in place . . . solid defense; Tarkenton, who had another big year, at quarterback; bookend wide receivers in Sammie White and Ahmad Rashad; Chuck Foreman in the backfield. So there they were, on the doorstep to the end zone in the first quarter of Super Bowl XI, having blocked a punt by Oakland's Ray Guy. With all their offensive weapons, the Vikings gave the ball to . . . Brent McClanahan? McClanahan's fumble prevented Minnesota from getting on the board first. Three plays later, Oakland back Clarence Davis ran 35 yards around left end, starting the Raiders on their first scoring drive. They'd never look back.

4. SUPER BOWL XII

Craig Morton picked up in Super Bowl XII right where he left off in Super Bowl V. Except this time he was at the helm of the Denver Broncos. Morton threw four interceptions in fifteen attempts (and he only completed four to his *own* team) before being benched for the immortal Norris Weese.

5. SUPER BOWL XV

Remember *Groundhog Day*, the movie with Bill Murray and Andie McDowell, in which Murray's character keeps reliving the same day over and over? That movie was made more than a decade after Super Bowl XV, when Eagles quarterback Ron Jaworski and Raiders linebacker Rod Martin had their own Groundhog Day. Martin picked off three Jaworski passes, on what looked like similar plays. These days, Martin wakes up and smiles when he thinks about that game. I'm sure when Jaworski dreams about that game, he wakes up in a nightmare.

6. SUPER BOWL XXVII

"Members of the AFC Champion Buffalo Bills will be giving away Super Bowl balls." No, that's not an ad for an autograph show. But it may as well have been printed in the Super Bowl XXVII program. Talk about freebies. The Bills turned the ball over *nine* times in their 52–17 loss to the Cowboys. That's hard to do if you try.

7. SUPER BOWL XXX

Right place, right time. That's cornerback Larry Brown's Super Bowl XXX—not to mention, his career—in a nutshell. In the second half of Super Bowl XXX, the Cowboys' defensive back picked off two errant Neil O'Donnell passes to set up Dallas touchdowns. On each play O'Donnell made bad reads and basically dropped the balls in Brown's lap. For this, Brown earned the game's MVP and signed a huge free agent contract with the Raiders. The only problem was, he wasn't a very good player; he had trouble covering receivers—a bad sign for someone who plays the cornerback position. His signing will go down as one of the biggest free agent flops of all time, possibly matched by O'Donnell's long-term deal with the Jets.

8. SUPER BOWL XXXVII

The Tampa Bay defense demanded to be put in the same league as the defensive lines of the Super Bowl champion Bears of 1985 and the Ravens of 2000, provided they won Super Bowl XXXVII. Well, the Bucs did win, thanks in great part to their five interceptions and a ferocious pass rush. But their defense still doesn't beat those other teams'.

9. SUPER BOWL XVIII

Yes, the Raiders again. This one boggles the mind, though. What were Joe Gibbs and Joe Theismann doing running a swing pass from their own 12-yard line with twelve seconds left in the half? Losing Super Bowl XVIII, apparently, as the little-known Jack Squirek grabbed one of the most famous interceptions in the game's history and ran it into the end zone to put the Raiders up 21–3. For all intents and purposes, the game was over at that point.

10. SUPER BOWL XVI

How do you outgain, score more touchdowns, and still get beaten by your opponent? Easy, when you fumble away a kickoff that leads to a field goal (Cincinnati running back Archie Griffin), throw an interception at the 5-yard line when you're about to score (quarterback Ken Anderson), and fumble away another scoring chance at the 8-yard line (wide receiver Cris Collinsworth). People seem to remember the 49ers' goal-line stand in the third quarter as the turning point in their win over the Bengals in Super Bowl XVI, but those three first-half turnovers had as much impact as anything in the second half.

Hollywood on My Mind

Hollywood loves a star athlete (and non-star athletes, if you consider the numerous movie roles of Brian Bosworth). Let's take a look at some of the Super Bowl stars that made a move to the big or small screen.

1. JOE NAMATH

Thank goodness Joe Namath can be remembered for winning Super Bowl III. His legend would certainly be tarnished if all anybody remembered about him was his starring role on the very-short-lived sitcom *The Waverly Wonders*. Remember his character Joe Casey, a high school basketball coach? No? Well, neither does anyone else.

2. FRED WILLIAMSON

Fred "The Hammer" Williamson talked a big game before Super Bowl I, and left the field on a stretcher, with his Chiefs getting blown out by the Packers. But who had the last laugh? Williamson has more than seventy film credits on his resume, including *M*A*S*H*. But he was best known for his action roles in a number of blaxploitation films of the seventies, among them *Hammer* (He even had a movie and a character named after himself!), *Black Caesar*, and *Hell Up in Harlem*.

3.   ED MARINARO

Colgate grad Ed Marinaro contributed little in the Vikings' loss in Super Bowl VIII, but he resurfaced a few years later as Officer Joe Coffey on the ground-breaking drama *Hill Street Blues*. That show may have been had one of the most athletically gifted casts in TV history. Michael Warren, once a star for John Wooden at UCLA, played officer Bobby Hill alongside Marinaro. Marinaro is probably more proud of his work on *Hill Street Blues* than he is of the TV movies *Amy Fisher: My Story,* in which he played Joey Buttafuoco, and *Police Woman Centerfold*.

4.   BRETT FAVRE

The driving force behind Green Bay's Super Bowl XXXI win, Brett Favre parlayed his success into a role in the Farrelly brothers' *There's Something About Mary*. He plays one of the many suitors for Cameron Diaz's Mary. Interestingly, another Super Bowl MVP, Steve Young, was considered for the role, but he reportedly declined due to his Mormon beliefs.

5.   BUBBA SMITH

What do you think Bubba Smith would like to forget more—his Colts' loss in Super Bowl III or his role as Sergeant Moses Hightower in six (yes, six!) *Police*

Academy movies? A veteran guest star on many shows from the seventies, including a memorable appearance as himself on *The Odd Couple*, Bubba should have known that signing on with a movie franchise anchored by Steve Guttenberg would be a bad career move.

6. FRAN TARKENTON

Former Vikings quarterback Fran Tarkenton more than held his own on ABC's wildly successful *That's Incredible*. A sort of reality show before there were reality shows, *That's Incredible* was co-hosted by Tarkenton, Cathy Lee Crosby, and John Davidson. Interestingly, Crosby had a long-term romantic fling with another Super Bowl quarterback, Joe Theismann of the Redskins.

7. TERRY BRADSHAW

Terry Bradshaw's four Super Bowl rings brought him to Hollywood's attention, and particularly to the attention of Burt Reynolds. Bradshaw was cast in three Reynolds movies in four years: *Hooper* (1978), *Smokey and the Bandit II* (1980), and *The Cannonball Run* (1981), but after that, the roles started to dry up. He did a number of guest spots on television series, including *Married . . . with Children* and *The Larry Sanders Show*, but later found his calling as a studio analyst with first CBS, then with FOX.

8. JOHN MATUSZAK

The poster boy for the wild-boy Raiders' championship teams in Super Bowls XI and XV, John "The Tooz" Matuszak carved a nice little niche in Hollywood before his tragic death. He was usually the big lug or the wild man. His first major role was in *North Dallas Forty*, a comedy/drama starring Nick Nolte and Mac Davis that was one of the better football movies ever made. His famous line in that role: "Every time I say it's a game, you say it's a business. Every time I say it's a business, you say it's a game." And though it's remembered very little these days, he starred in 1988's so-bad-it's-good *The Dirty Dozen: The Fatal Mission*, along with these other stars: Jeff Conaway of *Taxi* fame, Erik Estrada, Ernie Hudson, Ray "Boom Boom" Mancini, and Heather Thomas. You can't make this stuff up.

9. FRED DRYER

Fred Dryer was a starting defensive end for the Rams in their unlikely Super Bowl run in 1979, when they finished 9–7 but knocked off Dallas and Tampa Bay before losing to the Steelers in the big game. But just about everyone remembers Dryer for his role as Detective Sergeant Rick Hunter on the NBC series *Hunter*. The show, about a renegade Los Angeles detective who liked to play by his own rules (Don't they all?), lasted seven seasons, from 1984 through 1991.

10. DAN MARINO

Perhaps the greatest quarterback in NFL history, Dan Marino appeared in only one Super Bowl, and his movie career wasn't much to speak of, either. He played himself in the 1994 Jim Carrey comedy *Ace Ventura: Pet Detective*, in which someone has abducted the Dolphins' mascot (a real dolphin) just before the Super Bowl. Marino's coach, Don Shula, and teammates Pete Stoyanovich, Scott Mitchell, Marco Coleman, and Dwight Stephenson joined the cast as well.

That's *Mister* Perfect to You!

The 1972 Miami Dolphins may not have been the flashiest team, and they may not have been the most overpowering. But they are the only team in the Super Bowl era to go through the season undefeated, and then cap it off with a victory in the Super Bowl. People called them "No Names," but they were truly a collection of special personalities.

1. THE MOTIVATION

The 1972 Dolphins came into training camp stinging from the 24–3 thumping delivered to them by the Dallas Cowboys in Super Bowl VI. Miami was completely embarrassed, accounting for only ten first downs and setting a record for scoring futility with just three points. Up and down the roster, the Dolphins pointed to that loss as the starting point to their perfect season.

2. THE QUARTERBACKS

Quarterback Bob Griese had led Miami to Super Bowl VI in 1971 and was on his way to a Hall of Fame career. But in week five, he suffered a broken leg that sidelined him for the rest of the regular season. In stepped old warhorse Earl Morrall, who had played for Shula in Baltimore and, in fact, replaced Johnny Unitas in 1968 when Unitas was hurt. The team never lost a beat with Morrall, who guided the Dolphins through the remainder of the regular season. When Morrall faltered in the AFC Championship Game against Pittsburgh, Griese stepped back in and finished off the perfect season.

3. DON SHULA

In just a few short years, Don Shula turned the Dolphins from a laughingstock expansion team into an NFL dynasty. He then went on to become the winningest coach in NFL history. Stern yet compassionate, Shula had the respect of his team. One of the team leaders, running back Larry Csonka, felt that Shula was one of the primary reasons for the undefeated season: "The two superlatives that team had were pride and intelligence. And, oh yeah, Don Shula."

4. THE MINNESOTA GAME

The Dolphins had their share of close calls during the season, but their biggest scare came in week three, when they traveled to Minnesota. The Vikings led 14–6 midway through the fourth quarter, but Miami used Garo Yepremian's 51-yard field goal (his longest of the season) and a Griese touchdown pass to pull off a 16–14 win. The Dolphins were probably thanking the schedule makers for sending them to Minnesota early in the season, before the legendary frigid winters at Metropolitan Stadium.

5. **THE SCHEDULE**

You can only beat the teams they tell you to play, and the Dolphins couldn't control the fact that their schedule was pretty bad. It didn't help matters that no one else in their division had a winning record and that they only played two teams with winning records the whole season, beating Kansas City and the New York Giants, who both finished 8–6. They counted zero wins over playoff teams. Even a traditionally strong team like Minnesota stumbled to a .500 record in 1972. The members of the Dolphins bristle at the mention of the schedule, but a look at the facts indicates that it certainly didn't hurt their chances at going undefeated.

6. **THE RUNNING GAME**

They were completely opposite backs, but they complemented themselves perfectly. Mercury Morris could run as fast as anyone. Larry Csonka couldn't outrun the coaches but was a stocky, bruising back who was impossible to bring down. Both men averaged more than 5 yards per carry and went over 1,000 yards in 1972, aided by an outstanding offensive line. For a change of pace, coach Shula could send in Jim Kiick, who finished his year with 521 yards on the ground and had a knack for finding the end zone.

7. **THE PLAYOFFS**

Facing the enormous pressure of a perfect season, the Dolphins almost let it slip away in their divisional playoff game against the Cleveland Browns. More than 78,000 looked on as Miami used a touchdown on a blocked punt to take a 10–0 halftime lead. Despite hounding Cleveland quarterback Mike Phipps into five interceptions, the Cleveland ground game accounted for 165 yards, and when Phipps hit wide receiver Fair Hooker (I'm *not* making that name up) with a 27-yard touchdown pass, the Browns had a 14–13 fourth-quarter lead. The Dolphins responded with a drive that ended with a Kiick touchdown, and Miami escaped with a 20–14 win. The following week they traveled to Three Rivers Stadium to tackle the upstart Pittsburgh Steelers, fresh off their Immaculate Reception win over the Raiders. Once again, Miami looked unimpressive and trailed 10–7 in the third quarter. That's when Griese took over and led two touchdown drives, and Miami escaped with a 21–17 win.

8. THE POINT SPREAD

The Dolphins felt they were unappreciated for what they had done leading up to the Super Bowl, and there was a strong lack of respect from the national media especially. Then it happened. Las Vegas set their betting line for Super Bowl VII, and the Dolphins were . . . underdogs! Despite going undefeated, Miami was listed as a three-point underdog to the Redskins. Perhaps it was because of Miami's weak schedule, or maybe it was how impressive the Redskins were in dismantling the defending Super Bowl champion Cowboys in the NFC Championship Game. No matter to the Dolphins. They just used it as added motivation—as if they needed it!

9. THE LEGACY

No other team in the Super Bowl era has gone undefeated, and in the twenty-seven seasons since the NFL went to a sixteen-game schedule, only three teams have gone through a season with only one loss. As the years pass, the Dolphins' 1972 accomplishment seems more mythical and more and more likely never to happen again. But every year, there's one team that goes through the first part of their schedule without a loss, and inevitably, someone in the media will call upon the memory of the 1972 Dolphins. That's a nice legacy for a team to have.

10. THE CHAMPAGNE

More than thirty years have passed, but the members of that Miami team try to get together as often as possible to reminisce. Each year, they gather when the last undefeated team has lost. The corks are popped, the champagne flows, and the 1972 Dolphins toast another year as the only undefeated Super Bowl champion.

No, Really, You Were Great!

Perhaps the only title that is better than Super Bowl champion is Super Bowl MVP. But sometimes a player puts in a great performance, only to be outdone by a teammate (or in some cases, an opponent). Here are the best performances by players who did not win the Super Bowl MVP award.

1. TIM SMITH

A Super Bowl–record 204 yards rushing, two touchdowns, and a 9.3–yards per carry average. One of his touchdowns went for 58 yards. Seems like a lock for the MVP, right? Well, not so fast. Redskins rookie Tim Smith ate up the Broncos' defense in Super Bowl XXII, but his quarterback, Doug Williams, outdid him, throwing for 340 yards and four touchdowns in their 42–10 win.

2. THURMAN THOMAS

The best player on the field in Super Bowl XXV was on the losing team. Thurman Thomas rushed for 135 yards (a 9-yard average) and caught five passes for an additional 55 yards. Had the Bills won the game, he would have been a lock pick for the MVP. In fact, an argument can be made that Thomas deserved the award win or lose. So, Thomas lost out on the award when the Bills missed their last second kick. That's just another reason to complain about Scott Norwood.

3. LARRY CSONKA

Larry Csonka was the Dolphins' battering ram in Super Bowl VII. He pounded the Redskins for 112 hard-earned yards, including a punishing 49-yard run in the third quarter that left a handful of Washington defenders crying for mercy. But the MVP went to safety Jake Scott, who had two interceptions. Csonka did come back in Super Bowl VIII to win the award versus the Vikings.

4. GARY SANDERS

See Tim Smith, above. Gary Sanders, a Redskins receiver, caught nine passes for 193 yards and two touchdowns (including an 80-yarder) in Super Bowl XXII. So if you're keeping score, that's three individuals who had unbelievable performances for the Redskins. Nice job by the Broncos' defense!

5. CLARENCE DAVIS

This one is a little puzzling. In Super Bowl XI Oakland running back Clarence Davis rushed for 137 yards on just sixteen carries. Those numbers are good, though admittedly not overwhelming, but the MVP went to Raiders' wide receiver Fred Biletnikoff, who caught just four passes. Granted, three of his catches led to scores, but why him over Davis or even teammate Dave Casper, who had four catches and a touchdown?

6. JOHN STALLWORTH

The Steelers' wide receiver deserves recognition for his performance in Super Bowl XIV. Trailing the upstart Rams 19–17 early in the fourth quarter, John Stallworth grabbed a long bomb from Terry Bradshaw on a third-and-eight play and raced into the end zone for a 73-yard touchdown. Later in the quarter, he caught a 45-yard pass on a similar play, a reception that set up the touchdown that iced the game. Stallworth's two catches were the most important offensive plays in the Steelers' fourth Super Bowl win.

7. RAY WERSCHING

A kicker as Super Bowl MVP? Ray Wersching did not hit a game-winning field goal or boom kickoffs out of the end zone. But he did kick four field goals (still a Super Bowl record), and his trick squib kickoffs twice befuddled the Bengals in the second quarter, which helped the 49ers take a 20–0 lead into halftime. On the first, Cincinnati return man David Verser couldn't handle it, recovering at last on the 2-yard line. The poor field position enabled San Francisco to get the ball back and kick a field goal late in the half. On the ensuing kickoff, Archie Griffin couldn't handle the ball, and the 49ers recovered and kicked a field goal on the last play of the half.

8. MICHAEL PITTMAN

Michael Pittman had been a disappointment for the Buccaneers in his first year in Tampa Bay. Much was expected when he arrived from the Arizona Cardinals, but he did not have a single 100-yard rushing game during the regular season. But in Super Bowl XXXVII, he was Tampa Bay's best offensive player. He rushed twenty-nine times for 124 yards, and he was most important in the first half when Tampa Bay took over the game, running at will on the Raiders' defense.

9. JOE MONTANA

You may be wondering how a guy who won three Super Bowl MVP Awards could end up on this list, but listen to these numbers: twenty-three of thirty-six for 357 yards and two touchdowns, the second of which capped a 92-yard game-winning drive. This was Super Bowl XXIII, and Joe Montana lost the MVP voting to his teammate Jerry Rice, who caught eleven passes for 215 yards. Ironically, this leads us to . . .

10. JERRY RICE

In Super Bowl XXIX against the Chargers, Jerry Rice hauled in ten balls for 149 yards and three touchdowns. But the 1995 game might be better named the "Steve Young show." Young finally emerged from the shadow cast by Montana to win his first Super Bowl, tossing six touchdown passes along the way. As if throwing for 325 yards wasn't enough, Young scrambled for 49 yards rushing to lead the 49ers. The seven offensive touchdowns scored by San Francisco tied a record set by the Niners in Super Bowl XXIV.

Jon SooHoo

Jerry Rice's ten receptions and three touchdowns were not enough to earn MVP honors in Super Bowl XXIX. His quarterback, Steve Young, took home the award.

Big Name, Bad Game

Everyone wants to be a star in the Super Bowl. But even stars sometimes have bad games on Super Sunday.

1. THURMAN THOMAS

In the Buffalo Bills' second Super Bowl appearance, Thurman Thomas had one of his worst games as a pro. Just a year earlier, in Super Bowl XXV, he was the best player on the field in the Bills' loss to the New York Giants, but in Super Bowl XXVI against the Redskins everything went wrong for Thomas. He missed the first series of the game because he couldn't find his helmet, and it may have been better had he never found it. He finished the game with just 13 rushing yards on ten carries, as the Redskins toppled the Bills, 37–24.

2. THURMAN THOMAS

Really, there's no intention of making fun of Thurman Thomas, but his performance in Super Bowl XXVII was just as bad as his performance in Super Bowl XXVI. This time it was the Dallas Cowboys who shut down the versatile running back, holding him to just 19 yards on eleven carries in their 52–17 win. He did score a touchdown that gave the Bills a brief 7–0 lead in the first quarter, but he was also stopped at the 1-yard line during a second-quarter goal-line stand.

3. JOE THEISMANN

Joe Theismann was the 1983 NFL Most Valuable Player, and he led the Redskins' record-setting offense into Super Bowl XVIII, where they hoped to become the fifth team to win back-to-back Super Bowls. But the Los Angeles Raiders' defense frustrated Theismann, pressuring him into a well-below-average game: he finished just sixteen for thirty-five, for 264 yards and two interceptions. The Redskins scored only nine points and were beaten soundly, 38–9.

4. JOHN RIGGINS

One thing the Redskins counted on was that even when the passing game did not click, they could always give the ball to Riggo, who would eat up the yards for them. Running back John Riggins came into Super Bowl XVIII looking to repeat his MVP performance from Super Bowl XVII, but the Raiders gave him no running room. On twenty-six carries he could muster only 64 yards.

5. FRAN TARKENTON

Pittsburgh's Steel Curtain had a great game in Super Bowl IX at the expense of Vikings quarterback Fran Tarkenton. Tarkenton threw for close to 2,600 yards during the regular season, but the Steelers had other ideas. Their pressure forced Tarkenton to complete only eleven of twenty-six passes for a paltry 102 yards. Of those eleven completions, only one (one!) went to a wide receiver. It's no surprise then, that the Vikings were unable to muster an offensive touchdown or that they were defeated, 16–6.

6. CHUCK FOREMAN

Tarkenton's backfield mate with the Vikings, Chuck Foreman, rushed for 777 yards during the 1974 regular season, then added 204 yards in two playoff games. But he fell victim to the stingy Pittsburgh defense in Super Bowl IX as well, gaining just 18 yards on twelve carries—and 12 of those yards came on one rush. He wasn't much better in Minnesota's Super Bowl VIII loss to the Dolphins with only 18 yards on seven carries.

7. JIM MARSHALL

Jim Marshall was a long-time stalwart on the defensive line of the Minnesota Vikings. He played in 282 consecutive games in his career and had his number 70 retired by the Vikings. But in Super Bowl XI against the Oakland Raiders, he may as well have worn 00 because that would have matched his production. Lined up against Hall of Fame left tackle Art Shell, Marshall put up goose eggs on the stat sheet. He had no tackles and no sacks, and accounted for no takeaways. The Raiders easily handled the rest of the Minnesota defense as well in their 32–14 win, but Marshall's zeroes were most glaring.

8. MARSHALL FAULK

In 2001 running back Marshall Faulk accounted for more than 2,100 yards from the line of scrimmage. He led the St. Louis Rams into their second Super Bowl in three seasons, where they faced the New England Patriots. And the Patriots' defense was waiting. Faulk could rush for only 76 yards, and he caught four balls for only 54 yards—well below his season averages. The Rams went on to lose the game, 20–17.

9. RICH GANNON

Rich Gannon entered Super Bowl XXXVII against the Tampa Bay Buccaneers hoping to put an exclamation point on an MVP season. The Raiders' quarterback was a picture of precision and perfection with his short passing game . . . until he ran into the Tampa Bay defense. Gannon threw the ball forty-four times, completing twenty-four for 272 yards, but he was hounded by a fierce pass rush and sacked five times. He threw a Super Bowl–record five interceptions, three of which were returned for touchdowns.

10. WILBERT MONTGOMERY

Wilbert Montgomery was the Eagles' leading rusher in the 1980 Super Bowl season, gaining 778 yards on the ground. He was most impressive in the NFC Championship Game versus Dallas at Veterans Stadium, during which he ran for 194 yards. So, he entered Super Bowl XV against the Raiders hoping to continue his magic carpet ride, but the Raiders' defense would have no part of it. Montgomery was held to just 44 yards rushing, and while he accumulated 91 yards receiving, most of them came after the Raiders had built up a big lead. The Eagles never really threatened in their 27–10 loss.

Hail to the Chief
(No, Not Hank Stram)

It's impossible to overstate the importance of coaching in the NFL, so it's appropriate that the trophy awarded to the Super Bowl champion is named after one of the greatest coaches of all time: Vince Lombardi. Here are some of the coaches who made history in the Super Bowl.

1. VINCE LOMBARDI

You weren't expecting someone else, were you? After Vince Lombardi's teams dominated the first two Super Bowls, he was carried off the field for the last time. "This is the best way to leave a football field," he was quoted as saying. Although there was a definite love-hate relationship between Lombardi and his players, one thing was certain: They all respected him.

2. CHUCK NOLL

If Chuck Noll smiled more than four times in his career as head coach with the Steelers, I'd like to see the evidence. I imagine his only four smiles coincided with the Steelers' four Super Bowl championships. To put Noll's accomplishments in perspective, keep these facts in mind: No other coach has won four Super Bowls; in their first forty years of existence, the Steelers did not win any NFL championships; and since Noll has left Pittsburgh, the Steelers have not won any NFL championships.

3. JOE GIBBS

Joe Gibbs won three Super Bowls in four appearances between 1982 and 1991. But the remarkable thing about Gibbs, which separates him from a coach like Mike Shanahan, for instance, is that he won all three with different quarterbacks. Those quarterbacks—Joe Theismann, Doug Williams, and Mark Rypien—were good players but hardly all-time greats, and credit for their success can be attributed only to Gibbs's brilliant offensive game plans. In 2004 the Redskins returned to the past, coaxing Gibbs out of retirement to fill their head-coaching vacancy.

4. BILL WALSH

Whenever you hear the phrase "West Coast offense," you should take a moment to remember Bill Walsh. The one-time understudy to the legendary Paul Brown incorporated an open, short-passing game when he became head coach of the 49ers. In just three seasons he went from a 2–14 record to 13–3 and a championship in Super Bowl XVI. He won three Super Bowls without a loss, and he may have won a fourth if not for some questionable officiating in the fourth quarter of the 1983 NFC Championship Game (but that's another story). He went out victorious in his last NFL game, San Francisco's 20–16 win over Cincinnati in Super Bowl XXIII.

Jon SooHoo

Bill Walsh, the head coach and architect of three
Super Bowl champions with the San Francisco 49ers.

5. TOM LANDRY

He was stoic, he had a brilliant offensive mind, and he looked great in a fedora. Tom Landry guided his Dallas Cowboys to five Super Bowls in the 1970s, winning twice. But all of his Super Bowl losses were close games and could have gone either way—the Cowboys actually led in the fourth quarter of two of them. Looking at his overall career, you realize his two championship rings easily could have been five or six if the ball had bounced the right way in a few big games: the Ice Bowl, Super Bowl V, the Dwight Clark catch game, to name a few. Like the Cowboys or hate them, Landry was one of the most recognizable faces in the NFL during his nearly three-decade career in Dallas.

6. BILL PARCELLS

Bill Parcells nearly lost his job after one season as a head coach—a disastrous 3–12–1 campaign with the 1983 New York Giants. But general manager George Young decided to stick with him. Good thing for Giants fans that he did. By 1986 he'd won his—and the Giants'—first Super Bowl, 39–20 over the Denver Broncos. By 1990 his legend as a great coach was assured when his G-Men upset the heavily favored Buffalo Bills, 20–19, in Super Bowl XXV. But the man they call "The Tuna" didn't stop there. In 1996 he became just the second coach to lead two franchises to the Super Bowl, when he brought the New England Patriots to Super Bowl XXXI, where the favored Green Bay Packers beat them. Don't bet against Parcells making it back to the big game with his current franchise reclamation project, the Dallas Cowboys.

7. DON SHULA

Don Shula has lost four Super Bowls as a head coach, a dubious record he shares with three others. But this is rarely mentioned in discussing Shula's career. Well, when you're the NFL's all-time winningest coach, you've won two Super Bowls in dominant fashion, you coached the only undefeated Super Bowl champion in history, and you were the first to coach two different teams to the Super Bowl, you've earned the right for people to overlook your (few) shortcomings.

8. WEEB EWBANK

And you thought the only Wilbur you knew was that dope on *Mr. Ed*. Wilbur "Weeb" Ewbank makes the list because he coached the Jets in Super Bowl III. It doesn't matter if his career record was only one game over .500 and that his teams only won ten games or more twice in twenty seasons. But as the winning coach in the second-biggest game in league history (Super Bowl III), you earn your place in history. Oh, and the biggest game in league history? Weeb won that one, too, the 1958 NFL Championship Game, when his Colts beat the New York Giants.

9. DICK VERMEIL

It's not all that remarkable that Dick Vermeil has led two different franchises to Super Bowls. What is remarkable is that, after retiring from burnout two seasons after leading the Philadelphia Eagles to a loss in Super Bowl XV, he sat out fifteen seasons and returned to coaching with the St. Louis Rams. After only three seasons at the helm, his Rams beat the Tennessee Titans in Super Bowl XXXIV.

10. BUD GRANT

It is a terrible shame that Bud Grant will be most remembered as a coach who lost four Super Bowls. From 1969 through 1976, his teams averaged eleven wins, but they could never get over the top in January's big game. It doesn't help his legacy that his teams lost Super Bowls IV, VIII, IX, and XI by a combined score of 95–34 and never led in any of the games.

Taking the
Super Step

There's no better path to becoming an NFL head coach than climbing the rungs from offensive or defensive coordinator for a Super Bowl team. Many have taken this super step, but they have found that head-coaching success is not guaranteed.

1. BILL ARNSPARGER

As defensive coordinator of the Dolphins under Don Shula, Bill Arnsparger turned the No Name defense into a feared unit. Following Miami's back-to-back titles in Super Bowls VII and VIII, Arnsparger left Shula, with whom he had worked since Shula's time with the Colts, to become the head coach of the New York Giants. He lasted just two and a half seasons, compiling a record of 7–28, but things worked out well for Arnsparger. He returned to his pal Shula and worked as his defensive coordinator until 1983, helping to develop the Killer Bees defense. His final year as an NFL assistant was in 1994, when he led the San Diego defense to Super Bowl XXIX.

2. MIKE HOLMGREN

Mike Holmgren was the offensive coordinator for the most explosive performance in Super Bowl history, San Francisco's 55–10 dismantling of Denver in Super Bowl XXIV. The victory got him the attention of NFL front office types, and in 1992 he was hired to succeed Lindy Infante in Green Bay. Soon the Packers became playoff fixtures, and in 1996 Holmgren led the Pack to their third Super Bowl championship, behind quarterback Brett Favre.

3. NORV TURNER

Fresh off two straight Super Bowl championships with the Cowboys in 1992 and 1993, offensive coordinator Norv Turner left Big D to take the head coaching position with the archrival Washington Redskins. Performing in the shadow cast by former- (and future-) coach Joe Gibbs, Turner had an up-and-down seven year stint with the 'Skins. They finished with four winning seasons but made the playoffs just once, in 1999. Turner learned that being a head man is another world from being a coordinator and that having Heath Shuler and Gus Frerotte (two of his quarterbacks with Washington) is not the same as having Troy Aikman. Following the 2003 season, Al Davis hired Turner as the head coach of the Oakland Raiders.

4. DAVE WANNSTEDT

The defensive counterpart to Turner under Coach Jimmy Johnson at Dallas, Dave Wannstedt also left the Cowboys following the 1993 season. He was named coach of the Chicago Bears and spent six seasons on the sideline at Soldier Field. Despite being named 1994 NFC Coach of the Year and leading the Bears to a wild-card win over the Vikings in Minnesota, his overall record with Chicago was a disappointing 41–57. Wannstedt turned up in Miami to assist Johnson with the Dolphins. One year later he became the fourth head coach in Dolphins history, a position he holds at the time of this writing.

5. BUDDY RYAN

Buddy Ryan was the loud, take-no-bunk defensive coordinator for the 1985 Chicago Bears. It's a small wonder that he was wanted as a head coach by other franchises. But Ryan was no one-year wonder. In fact, he was a long-time assistant who had been on Weeb Ewbank's Jets staff in Super Bowl III. Ryan left Chicago to take over the Philadelphia Eagles and, boy, did he ever. The Eagles took on their coach's mean, tough, and (some would say) dirty personality, and during his five-year tenure, he led Philadelphia to the playoffs three times. Ryan never won a playoff game with Philly, however, and he left following the 1990 season. Later he became defensive coordinator of the Oilers, where he infamously got into a fistfight on the sideline with offensive coach Kevin Gilbride during a game against the Jets. He also spent two dismal seasons leading the Arizona Cardinals in 1994 and 1995.

6. JOE BUGEL

As the offensive line coach, then offensive coordinator, and later assistant head coach of the Redskins under Joe Gibbs, Joe Bugel helped build the Hogs' offensive line and orchestrated the Fun Bunch offense of 1983, which set a then-NFL record for points scored. He was on the sideline for two Super Bowl championships and was one of Gibbs's trusted confidantes. In 1990 he went west to take over the Phoenix Cardinals, but as many others have learned, trying to win with that Arizona franchise is futile. He finished up a four-year term with a record of 20–44. Later, in 1997, Al Davis hired Bugel to help turn around the Raiders. And Bugel did. He made them worse, finishing 4–12 in his only season as head coach. In 2004 Bugel rejoined the Redskins as assistant head coach when Joe Gibbs came out of retirement.

7. BILL BELICHICK

Bill Belichick began his career just out of college working for the Baltimore Colts. By work ethic alone, he's become one of the most respected coaches in all of football. He first rose to prominence in New York, as the defensive coordinator for two Giants' Super Bowl championship teams. Following Super Bowl XXV, Art Modell hired him to take over for Bud Carson in Cleveland. He had a rough go of it with the Browns. Belichick never seemed comfortable in front of the media, the team didn't win enough, and then he had the audacity to bench city favorite Bernie Kosar for Vinny Testaverde. In 1994, however, the Browns put it all together and went to the playoffs. Things were in place for a great 1995 until Modell decided to relocate the team to Baltimore. The distractions from the impending move became too much, and following the season, Belichick was let go. His record in Cleveland was 37–45.

But Belichick wasn't through. He hooked up with his old head coach, Bill Parcells in New England, and stayed with him for a move back to New York, where he became defensive coordinator for the Jets. After three years, and an aborted decision to accept New York's coaching job, he returned to the Patriots. Belichick must have learned from whatever mistakes he made in Cleveland because he's won two Super Bowls in his time in New England.

8. JOHN FOX

John Fox rode the Giants' magical run to the Super Bowl in 2000 to a head-coaching job in Carolina two seasons later. The Giants' defensive coordinator under Jim Fassel, he coached the Panthers to Super Bowl XXXVIII, where he met the Patriots and Bill Belichick. That contest featured two former Giants defensive coordinators going head-to-head with each other. Three other former Giants coordinators have gone on to coach other teams in the Super Bowl. Their names? Lombardi, Landry, and Parcells.

9. MARVIN LEWIS

A bit of an uproar followed the 2000 season because Marvin Lewis was unable to get a head-coaching job. Lewis was the mastermind of the Ravens' defense that set a record for fewest points allowed in a single season and that thoroughly dominated four opponents in the postseason (one offensive touchdown allowed) to win Super Bowl XXXV. But because of NFL rules, teams with a coaching opening could not speak to candidates until their season ended. By that time, all but one of the available jobs was filled. But Lewis kept at it, helping to guide the Ravens to the playoffs the following season. In 2002 Redskins owner Dan Snyder opened the vault to bring Lewis in as his defensive coordinator under Steve Spurrier. Finally, Lewis was hired to coach the Cincinnati Bengals in 2003 and, in his first season, guided the long-dormant franchise back to respectability.

10. GREGG WILLIAMS

Gregg Williams was the whiz responsible for the Tennessee Titans' defense in Super Bowl XXXIV. His success with the Titans led him to Buffalo, where he had three rather lackluster seasons as head coach. He was fired following the 2003 season, but thanks to Dan Snyder's largesse, he joined the Redskins as a defensive coach under Joe Gibbs at a salary *increase* over his job in Buffalo. In case you're counting, four coaches on this list (Turner, Bugel, Lewis, and Williams) have at one time worked for Snyder, which proves either that there's no job security with the Redskins or that coaches love the man's money.

Brothers-in-Pads

Football is a family game. Parents pass their love of the game along to their children. Brothers play against each other in heated backyard games, dreaming that one day they may play in the biggest game of them all. Here are some of the lucky families who have had two members play in the Super Bowl.

1. THE BAHRS

Matt Bahr always seemed to follow in the footsteps of his brother Chris. Chris had a solid collegiate career as a kicker for Penn State, and when his brother graduated, Matt kicked for Joe Paterno's team. After Chris went to the NFL, Matt followed. But when it comes to the Super Bowl, Matt got there first, as a rookie kicker for Pittsburgh's fourth Super Bowl championship team. Chris didn't have to wait much longer to get a ring of his own. He handled the placekicking chores for the Raiders just one season later, in their 27–10 win over the Eagles. Both brothers added rings later in their career—Chris again with the Raiders in Super Bowl XVIII, and Matt with the Giants in Super Bowl XXV.

2. THE DORSETTS

Hall of Fame running back Tony Dorsett won a Super Bowl with the Dallas Cowboys in his rookie year, 1977. Twenty-two years later, he became the only Super Bowl player whose son also played in the big game when Anthony Dorsett suited up for the Tennessee Titans against the St. Louis Rams. Alas, Tony is the only one in the family to win the ring, as the Rams beat the Titans 23–16, but Anthony was involved in the pivotal play of his big game; he was beaten by St. Louis wide receiver Isaac Bruce on a 73-yard touchdown pass that provided the winning margin for the Rams.

3. THE BARBERS

Twins in the Super Bowl! Identical twins Tiki and Ronde Barber, who played together at the University of Virginia and are still active in the NFL, reached the Super Bowl within three seasons of each other. Tiki was the leading rusher for the New York Giants in their 34–7 loss to the Ravens in Super Bowl XXXV, while Ronde was a starter at cornerback for the Buccaneers in their win over the Raiders in Super Bowl XXXVII. Ronde was one of the big reasons his team was even in the game, scoring a big touchdown on an interception return in the NFC Championship Game against the Eagles.

4. THE MICHAELS

The first time that two brothers faced each other on opposite sidelines in a Super Bowl was in January

1969. Lou Michaels was the Colts kicker in Super Bowl III, a game he'd like to forget. Not only did he miss two field goals, but he also got into a pregame war of words with the Jets' Joe Namath, which didn't work out too well. To top it all off, his brother, Walt, helped put together New York's defensive game plan as an assistant with the Jets. Walt Michaels later had a six-year run as the Jets' head coach.

5. THE TUIASOSOPOS

The Dorsetts are the only father-son combination to play in the Super Bowl, but the Tuiasosopos—father Manu and son Marcus—both were in uniform for the game. Manu started at defensive tackle for the 49ers in their 38–16 win over the Dolphins in Super Bowl XIX, recording one of their four sacks of Dan Marino. Marcus was the backup quarterback for the Raiders in Super Bowl XXXVII but did not play in their loss to Tampa Bay. Considering how poorly Rich Gannon played in that game, Coach Bill Callahan could have given Marcus a shot.

6. THE BLACKWOODS

Could anything be better for two brothers? Not only did Lyle Blackwood and his younger brother Glenn each make the Super Bowl, but they also did it as team-mates, and they started alongside each other in the defensive backfield for the Miami Dolphins in Super Bowls XVII and XIX. Well, winning one of the games could have been better, but the Blackwoods had respectable games. Two vital cogs in Miami's Killer Bees defense, Lyle had sixteen tackles, an interception, and a fumble recovery in the two games, while Glenn had five tackles and one pass defensed.

7. THE GRIFFINS

Archie Griffin left Ohio State with two Heisman Trophies and went to the Bengals with a lot of hype. Unfortunately, his college success never translated as a pro. A few years later his brother Ray followed Archie from Ohio State to Cincinnati, and both were key reserves for Cincinnati in Super Bowl XVI. However, Archie had a pivotal fumble in the game, and Ray had little impact on the defensive side, recording only one tackle.

8. THE FAHNHORSTS

Brothers Jim and Keith Fahnhorst each had long careers with the San Francisco 49ers. Both started in two Super Bowls, and they were teammates for four seasons. However, they never suited up together in the big game. Keith, a long-time offensive lineman, was so disgusted with the 49ers' losing ways that early in the 1981 season he demanded a trade. Fortunately for him, management ignored his plea. He went on to get two rings with the 49ers in Super Bowl XVI and Super Bowl XIX. Jim was an inside linebacker in the Niners' wins in Super Bowl XXIII and XXIV.

9. THE HILGENBERGS

Wally Hilgenberg spent a long career as a linebacker with the Vikings, playing behind the powerful Purple People Eaters' defensive line and starring on four teams that reached the big game. Wally's teams never won a ring, but nephew Jay, a ten-year center with the Bears, started for Chicago's Super Bowl XX win.

10. **KEYSHAWN JOHNSON AND SAMARI ROLLE**

Keyshawn Johnson, the loudmouthed wide receiver, starred for the Tampa Bay Buccaneers in their Super Bowl XXXVII win over the Raiders. Rolle, his cousin, was a starter in the defensive backfield for the Tennessee Titans in Super Bowl XXXIV, when the Titans lost to the Rams. A third cousin is waiting in the wings: Charles Johnson, the wide receiver for the Bengals who may have a bigger mouth than Keyshawn.

Now That's Entertainment!

Attending a Super Bowl is no longer just sitting down for a game. There're hours of pregame festivities, a flashy, extra-long halftime show, and even a postgame concert. As you'll see from the list below, the people who have performed at the Super Bowl run the gamut of world-renowned superstars and some little-known acts.

1. **U2**

It was the first Super Bowl in the post–9/11 era. Super Bowl XXXVI in New Orleans was the site for the best halftime show to date, one to which all shows from this point on will be compared. U2 had long been one of the most popular bands in the world, and their heartfelt performance of the hits "Beautiful Day" and "Where the Streets Have No Name," as the names of all the victims of the terrorist attacks on the World Trade Center and the Pentagon scrolled on a big screen behind the stage, is one that still resonates to this day.

2. UP WITH PEOPLE

What the heck was the NFL thinking? Up With People were the halftime performers for three Super Bowls in the 1970s and 1980s. Who were Up With People? Picture the cast of Coca-Cola's "I'd Like to Teach the World to Sing" commercial remade with bright new-age-type outfits. In other words, Up With People was a band that was way out of place at a football game. But there they were, at Super Bowls X, XIV, and XX, dancing around in celebrations of the bicentennial, the big band era, and the future. It's believed that following their final appearance Pete Rozelle said, "Three words I never want to hear ever again: Up With People."

3. MICHAEL JACKSON

If only the NFL knew then what they know now. At Super Bowl XXVII Michael Jackson "and local children" were the featured act for the Heal the World halftime show. It was January 1993, and Jackson was still one of the biggest stars on the planet, so it was seemingly a great "get" for the people putting together the entertainment. But not long after, the first of many allegations came down against the Gloved One. On another note, the NFL probably wishes they also had a mulligan on their choice for the 1993 pregame coin flip: O. J. Simpson.

4. BON JOVI

The New Jersey rockers have been at the top of the rock world for two decades thanks to popular power ballads like "Livin' on a Prayer," "You Give Love a Bad Name," "Runaway," and "Wanted: Dead or Alive." They've also been involved with a number of NFL events during the last few seasons: They sang an acoustic "God Bless America" before the NFL games on September 23, 2001, and they were part of the 2002 season kickoff concert in Times Square. They became the first postgame musical act following Super Bowl XXXVII, when they performed their hit "It's My Life" before the presentation of the Vince Lombardi Trophy.

5. CHERYL LADD

No, that's not a misprint. With Super Bowl XIV in southern California (at the Rose Bowl), the NFL brought in a hot-at-the-moment celebrity to sing the National Anthem. And Cheryl Ladd fit the bill. She was a star on *Charlie's Angels*, and well, that's all she was. Who knew she had more talent than just jiggling around in a bikini? No one knew, before she sang. And they didn't afterwards, either.

6. STYX AND STING

For Super Bowl XXXV in Tampa, the theme of the pregame show was "Life is super in central Florida." Not if you had to watch Styx perform. And the truly sad thing is that these has-beens actually performed with Sting. How did Sting get stuck being involved in this? The organizers of this pregame performance also had the brilliant idea to bring Britney Spears, Aerosmith, NSYNC, and Melissa Etheridge onto the stage for the halftime show. Was there no one with any sense putting this show together?

7. KISS

I suppose it would have been more impressive to get KISS involved in the Super Bowl back in the seventies, when their popularity was sky high. But before Super

Bowl XXXIII in 1999? The face-painting rockers took part in a pregame show celebrating Caribbean cruises (and yes, the game was played in Miami). I'd hate to think they were that desperate for the exposure to have agreed to this.

8. NEW KIDS ON THE BLOCK

Here's another situation where the NFL got the hot act of the moment. The New Kids on the Block were the original boy band, who paved the way for later groups including 98 Degrees, NSYNC, and the Backstreet Boys. Yes, the New Kids on the Block had the "Right Stuff" for the NFL in January 1991 as the headline act in Disney's halftime show, "A Small World Salute to Twenty-five Years of the Super Bowl."

9. JANET JACKSON AND JUSTIN TIMBERLAKE

With CBS broadcasting Super Bowl XXXVIII, Viacom thought it would be a good act of synergy to turn the halftime show over to their corporate brothers at MTV. Part of the pageantry included forty-something has-been Janet Jackson performing with boy-band veteran Justin Timberlake. With millions of people watching, Timberlake ripped at Ms. Jackson's top, in what certainly appeared to be part of the act, revealing Ms. Jackson's breast. Days of intrigue followed, with the NFL furious at both CBS and the performers (although they could just as easily have pointed the finger at themselves) and the performers claiming the incident was an accident. Later, Timberlake admitted that the act was prearranged but that he expected Ms. Jackson to be wearing a red bra. Timberlake apologized a week later at the Grammy Awards, which coincidentally were broadcast by CBS.

10. SUPER BOWL XXIX

How do you keep a crowd of over 70,000 entertained when the biggest game of the year is a wipeout? Easy. Hold a celebration honoring 150 years of Florida statehood, seventy-five years of the NFL, and twenty-five years of Monday Night Football (and yes, ABC was broadcasting the game). Throw in a flyover by an Air Force fighter squadron, a Miami dance troupe, Sergio Mendes, Joe Namath, and Hank Williams Jr. And now sprinkle in Kathie Lee Gifford, former Miss America Heather Whitestone, and add an Indiana Jones tribute with Tony Bennett, Miami Sound Machine, Arturo Sandoval, and Patti LaBelle. That might actually make you forget that Super Bowl XXIX was a 49–26 wipeout for the 49ers over the Chargers.

You Are
My Shining Star

The most visible and popular player on a football team is almost always the quarterback. It's generally accepted that you can't win the Super Bowl if you don't have a big-time quarterback, and historically that has been the case. To choose the best performances by a quarterback in the big game is not easy; just take a look at the list below.

1. PHIL SIMMS, SUPER BOWL XXI

In 1979 Giants fans booed when he was drafted in the first round out of Morehead State. In 1983 he lost his starting job when rookie head coach Bill Parcells chose to go with Scott Brunner at his quarterback. Phil Simms did not become entrenched as the Giants quarterback until the 1984 season, and it was just two years later that he had perhaps the best Super Bowl ever for a quarterback. In the Giants' 39–20 win over the Broncos, Simms completed twenty-two of twenty-five passes to eight different receivers, for 268 yards and three touchdowns. He completed every pass he attempted in a thirty-point second half.

Jon SooHoo

Phil Simms had a near-perfect day for the Giants
in their Super Bowl XXI win over the Broncos.

2. KURT WARNER, SUPER BOWL XXXIV

From a grocery store to NFL Europe to Super Bowl MVP. Happens every day, right? Kurt Warner played quarterback at Northern Iowa, spent one training camp as a backup to Brett Favre in Green Bay, and put in a little time with NFL Europe. His big opportunity came in the 1999 preseason when Rams starting quarterback Trent Green went down with an injury. Warner stepped in and led the unheralded Rams to the best record in the NFL and a trip to the Super Bowl. There, he threw for a Super Bowl–record 414 yards and two big touchdowns, including the game-winner in their 23–16 triumph, a 73-yard strike to wide receiver Isaac Bruce with 1:54 remaining.

3. STEVE YOUNG, SUPER BOWL XXIX

Steve Young had a long road to his first Super Bowl championship. His professional career began in the USFL, then he went to the NFL graveyard of Tampa Bay, before being traded to the 49ers. He then spent four years as a backup to Joe Montana, when an injury to Montana forced Young into the starting lineup. It took four years of playoff disappointments before Young guided San Francisco to the big game, and once he got there, he made the best of it. Young completed six touchdown passes and threw for 325 yards as the 49ers trounced the Chargers, 49–26.

4. JOE MONTANA, SUPER BOWL XXIV

Joe Montana's achievements in the Super Bowl are legendary. Only Terry Bradshaw matches his 4–0 record, and he saved one of his best performances for his last Super Bowl appearance. In Super Bowl XXIV he led the 49ers to the most lopsided win in the history of the game, a 55–10 destruction of the Denver Broncos. He completed twenty-two of twenty-nine passes for 297 yards and five touchdowns.

5. TERRY BRADSHAW, SUPER BOWL XIII

Terry Bradshaw took some ribbing from the Cowboys in the week leading up to Super Bowl XIII, and he took out his frustrations on the field. Despite a first-half fumble that Dallas linebacker Mike Hegman ran back for a touchdown, Bradshaw had a 318-yard passing day and connected on four touchdown passes. His 18-yarder to wide receiver Lynn Swann midway through the fourth quarter gave them a 35–17 lead and put the game out of reach.

6. DOUG WILLIAMS, SUPER BOWL XXII

Doug Williams came out of Grambling and led the lowly Tampa Bay Buccaneers to two playoff appearances, but then his career started to fizzle. Rescued by Joe Gibbs and the Redskins following Joe Theismann's retirement, Williams led Washington to Super Bowl XXII. Bombarded by questions about his status as the first African-American to lead his team to the Super Bowl, Williams responded with a virtuoso game-day performance. After an ankle injury put him down for a few plays in the first quarter, he caught fire. He completed just eighteen passes, but they went for 340 yards and four touchdowns, enough to earn him the game's MVP.

7. TROY AIKMAN, SUPER BOWL XXVII

The Dallas Cowboys went to five of the first thirteen Super Bowls, but it took them fourteen seasons to get back again. Instead of Tom Landry and Roger Staubach, Troy Aikman and Jimmy Johnson were at the helm. The first overall pick in the 1989 draft, he suffered through a 1–15 season as a rookie, but gradually the Cowboys improved, and after a playoff appearance in 1991, Dallas made it to Super Bowl XXVII the following year. In no small part due to Aikman, the Cowboys blew out the Buffalo Bills 52–17. Aikman had four touchdown passes and tossed for 273 total yards.

8. JOHN ELWAY, SUPER BOWL XXXIII

One year after exorcising the demons of Denver's Super Bowl past, John Elway led the Broncos to their second consecutive title in Super Bowl XXXIII, with a command performance in the final game of his career. Elway rushed for one touchdown and threw for 336 yards, including an 80-yard touchdown to Rod Smith, as the Broncos cruised past the Atlanta Falcons, 34–19.

9. JOE MONTANA, SUPER BOWL XIX

Joe Montana makes his second appearance on this list thanks to a superior performance in the 49ers' resounding 38–16 win over the Dolphins. He threw for 331 yards and three touchdowns and also rushed for 59 yards and another touchdown. That's 390 yards of total offense!

10. TERRY BRADSHAW, SUPER BOWL XIV

Terry Bradshaw picked up in Super Bowl XIV against the Rams where he left off the previous year against the Cowboys. Despite being intercepted three times in the first three quarters, Bradshaw still came up with the big plays when needed. He completed three second-half passes of 45 yards or more, two of them for touchdowns that put Pittsburgh ahead and the other to set up the score that iced the game.

It's a Kick

We've all heard the grumblings about kickers: "They're not part of the team." "They're not real football players." Usually, it's linemen who do most of the griping. But think about how often kickers affect the outcome of a game and the pressure of a big kick in the final minutes. Perhaps they ought to get treated with a little more respect in their own locker rooms. The Super Bowl has seen glory for some kickers, heartache for others, and slapstick comedy for one.

1. GARO YEPREMIAN

There's no way he could escape this list. Oh, Garo, what were you thinking? Your Dolphins had Super Bowl VII in the bag, with a 14–0 lead and just over two minutes remaining, when you trotted onto the field to attempt a game-clinching field goal. The kick was blocked. Oh well, your team still had a two-touchdown lead. But you had to pick it up and be a hero, didn't you? Well, we all know what happened. You tried to throw it, fumbled, and then watched as Washington's

Mike Bass raced the other way with the ball for a touchdown. OK, your team still won the game to cap off an undefeated season, and you made yourself a little celebrity (even appearing in a commercial for Ban deodorant), but here it is more than three decades later, and some of your teammates still hold a grudge against you for it. Was it all worth it, Garo?

2. JAN STENERUD

Jan Stenerud, who retired in 1985 after nineteen seasons, is the only placekicker in the NFL Hall of Fame. (George Blanda, who is also in the Hall, was a quarterback in addition to being a kicker.) When he called it quits, he was the all-time leader in field goals made, and three of his biggest came in Super Bowl IV, as his Kansas City Chiefs upset the heavily favored Minnesota Vikings, 23–7. On a sloppy turf, his 48-yarder in the first quarter gave the Chiefs a lead they didn't relinquish, and he added two more field goals and two extra points.

3. RAY WERSCHING

Ray Wersching had a great game in San Francisco's Super Bowl XVI win over the Cincinnati Bengals; in fact, an argument can be made that no 49er had a better game. He tied a Super Bowl record by going four-for-four in field goal opportunities, including two in the fourth quarter that iced the game after the Bengals had cut the lead to six points. In the second quarter his squib kickoff led to a fumble that the 49ers recovered, which set up another field goal. In two Super Bowls he did not miss a kick: He was five-for-five in field goals and seven-for-seven in extra points.

4. **ADAM VINATIERI**

Adam Vinatieri made the biggest kick in Super Bowl history when he hit a 48-yarder at the final gun to lead his New England Patriots to a Super Bowl XXXVI win over the St. Louis Rams, 20–17. Talk about a clutch kick! But this may not have been his most important kick in the postseason. Just two weeks before, in a driving snowstorm in Foxboro, he hit a 45-yarder in the final minute to tie the Oakland Raiders and send the game into overtime. Then he nailed a game-winner in the extra session. That's three enormous kicks in the course of three weeks. And how about doing it all again in two seasons? Yes, just a couple of years later, Vinatieri was on the big stage again, once more in a tie game late in Super Bowl XXXVIII, to kick the winning field goal as the Patriots knocked off the Panthers, 32–29.

5. **JIM O'BRIEN**

Jim O'Brien and Adam Vinatieri are the only two kickers to win a Super Bowl on a last second field goal. O'Brien is probably the most unlikely Super Bowl hero. He ended the wild, sloppy Super Bowl V with a 32-yard field goal, giving the Colts a 16–13 win over the Cowboys. That kick closed his rookie year, but O'Brien lasted only another two seasons with the Colts, including a dismal 1972, the year he hit just thirteen of thirty-one field goals. His career came to an end in 1973 with Detroit.

6. **KYLE RICHARDSON**

Do you ever expect a team to win when they have to punt ten times? Well, it happened in Super Bowl XXXV,

as the Baltimore Ravens trounced the New York
Giants, 34–7. Richardson dropped five of his punts
inside the Giants' 20-yard line, including one that land-
ed at the 1-yard line. With a great defense like the
Ravens had, field position was always important, and
Richardson always seemed to create a long field for
the opposition. In fact, in each of their postseason
games, Richardson had at least one punt downed
inside the opponents' 10-yard line.

7. MATT BAHR

Bahr is the answer to a fun Super Bowl trivia question:
Who is the only player to win a Super Bowl in the '70s
and the '90s but not in the '80s? As a rookie in 1979,
Bahr came out of Penn State and took over placekicking duties from long-time Steeler Roy Gerela. He
arrived in Pittsburgh in time for the Steelers' fourth
Super Bowl title. Then, following eight seasons with
the Cleveland Browns, Bahr went to the New York
Giants, just in time for the 1990 season. Bahr was
instrumental in New York's 20–19 win over the Bills in
Super Bowl XXV, kicking the 21-yard field goal in the
fourth quarter that gave the Giants their final score.

8. THE DALLAS COWBOYS

Clark, Fritsch, Herrera, Septien, Elliott, Murray, and
Boniol. This sounds like it could be an international
finance firm based somewhere in Zurich, but it's actu-
ally the lineup of placekickers used by the Dallas
Cowboys in their many Super Bowl appearances.
Seven kickers in eight Super Bowls! Mike Clark start-
ed the ball rolling as the kicker in Super Bowls V and
VI; he's the only man to kick in more than one Super
Bowl for Dallas. Interestingly, on two other occasions,

the Cowboys went to three Super Bowls in four years, and each time, they used a different kicker.

9. JIM TURNER

Jim Turner—who retired in the top ten of all-time career points scored—made three field goals for the New York Jets in their Super Bowl III upset over the Colts. Then, as a crusty veteran, he became the first kicker in Super Bowl history to kick for two different teams when he handled the placekicking chores for the Denver Broncos in Super Bowl XII. His 47-yard field goal didn't help the Broncos, though, as they were trounced by the Cowboys, 27–10.

10. JASON ELAM

Jason Elam shares the record for the longest regular season field goal—63 yards—and he kicked three field goals for the Broncos in their wins in Super Bowls XXXII and XXXIII. Among those kicks was a 51-yarder—on grass—in Denver's 31–24 Super Bowl XXXII win over Green Bay.

America's Team

No franchise has played in more Super Bowls than the Dallas Cowboys, who've played in eight of the thirty-eight games, and only the San Francisco 49ers can match Dallas's five championships. Few teams in all of sports elicit the kind of reaction the Cowboys do—from friend or foe. Their fans are rabid and bleed Cowboy silver and blue; those who despise the Cowboys do so with intensity, from the Dallas owner to the coaches to the players.

1. ROGER STAUBACH

Roger "the Dodger" Staubach quarterbacked the Cowboys to four of their Super Bowls in the 1970s, winning twice. He was an artist as a quarterback and was the master of the two-minute drill. Dallas fans remember that he was on the roster for Super Bowl V against the Colts but stayed on the bench as Craig Morton bumbled his way to a 16–13 defeat. In Staubach's two wins (Super Bowl VI versus Miami and Super Bowl XII versus Denver), he was masterful, throwing for three touchdowns without an interception. But in his two losses to Pittsburgh in Super Bowls X and XIII, he played a little fast and loose with the football. Yes, he did throw for five touchdowns, but he was also picked off four times and fumbled four times.

2. ED "TOO TALL" JONES

A monster defensive end, Ed "Too Tall" Jones stood six feet, eight inches tall and started three Super Bowls for the Cowboys. His sheer size disrupted opposing offenses. It's too bad more people remember him for an ill-advised foray into professional boxing and a failed attempt to make it in Hollywood, because he and Harvey Martin provided a pair of dominant pass-rushing defensive ends for the Cowboys. In Super Bowl XII he was part of the unit that terrorized the Broncos with three passes knocked down and a tackle for a loss. Then in Super Bowl XIII he recovered a fumble to set up a Dallas score and added two more tackles for losses.

3. CLIFF HARRIS AND CHARLIE WATERS

Cliff Harris and Charlie Waters were the same age and were almost the same size. They both hit hard and were known as ball hawks. They wore the same double-bar facemask on their helmets. They even wrote a book together, *Tales from the Dallas Cowboys*. Harris (number 43) played in five Pro Bowls; Waters (number 41), three. And they played alongside each other in the Dallas secondary for all five of their Super Bowls in the 1970s—Harris at free safety, and Waters on the strong side. Waters was on the field for two of the more controversial plays in Cowboys history: tight end John Mackey's touchdown off a double deflection for the Colts in Super Bowl V, and defensive back Bennie

Barnes's pass interference penalty on Pittsburgh's Lynn Swann in the fourth quarter of Super Bowl XIII. Harris was the more vocal of the two, notably talking trash with Swann in Super Bowl X and getting into a spat with Jack Lambert in the same game.

4. MARK WASHINGTON

The secondary for the Cowboys in the 1970s included future Hall of Famers Herb Adderley and Mel Renfro, the aforementioned Waters and Harris, as well as seasoned pros like Cornell Green. Small wonder, then, that the Steelers tried to zero in on cornerback Mark Washington during Super Bowl X. Washington had the unenviable task of being matched up with Pittsburgh wide receiver Lynn Swann. Swann caught only four balls, but his juggling 53-yarder with Washington draped all over him still makes highlight reels, and he beat Washington on the 64-yard touchdown in the fourth quarter that sealed the Steelers' win.

5. CHUCK HOWLEY

For all the talk about the great Dallas defense in the 1970s, you hear very little about Chuck Howley. An outside linebacker, he's overshadowed by the other great defensive starters for the Cowboys. Consider: In Super Bowl V the Cowboys started Bob Lilly, George Andrie, Lee Roy Jordan, Herb Adderley, Mel Renfro, and Cornell Green, yet it was Howley who emerged as the game's MVP. His two interceptions helped him become the only MVP recipient for a losing team. Not satisfied, he came back the next year and had another interception to go along with a fumble recovery. Both plays set up touchdowns in Dallas's 24–3 win over the Miami Dolphins.

6. TROY AIKMAN

Even though Troy Aikman led the Cowboys to three Super Bowl championships (only Terry Bradshaw and Joe Montana have more), his name isn't mentioned when the discussion turns to all-time great quarterbacks. The nagging perception—fair or unfair—of Aikman is that he was a really good quarterback, given all the tools with which to work. Aikman was flawless in Super Bowl XXVII, as he threw four touchdown passes and won the game's MVP. He followed that up with a win in the big game the next year. Not bad for a guy who suffered a concussion the week before Super Bowl XXVIII and still has trouble remembering the game that year. And he finished off the Steelers in Super Bowl XXX to become the only quarterback to win three Super Bowls in four years.

7. JIMMY JOHNSON

He's a college guy, they said, when Jimmy Johnson came to the Cowboys after coaching at the University of Miami. He's too slick to make it here, they said about the coach with the perfectly coiffed hair. But Johnson had the last laugh, turning a 1–15 squad in his first year into Super Bowl champions just four seasons later, becoming the first Dallas coach to win the Super Bowl since Tom Landry fifteen years earlier.

8. CHARLES HALEY

Charles Haley gets special notice here for winning three Super Bowls with the Cowboys in the early 1990s. Add that to the two he won with San Francisco in 1988 and 1989, and you have the Super Bowl's only five-time champion. He is also the only link between two dominant dynasties: Bill Walsh's 49ers and Jimmy

Johnson's Cowboys. Here's an interesting bit of trivia about Haley's five Super Bowl rings: All five came in an eight-year span, and he won them with four head coaches (Walsh, Johnson, George Seifert, and Barry Switzer).

9. LEON LETT

Does the name Don Beebe ring a bell? Defensive lineman Leon Lett is best remembered for being stripped of the football at the 1-yard line by the Bills' receiver during the fourth quarter of Super Bowl XXVII. With the game well out of reach, Beebe chased down Lett, who had recovered a Frank Reich fumble, in one of the most incredible hustle plays in Super Bowl history.

10. JAY NOVOCEK

Completely overshadowed by offensive teammates Troy Aikman, Emmitt Smith, Michael Irvin, and Alvin Harper (heck, even Moose Johnston), tight end Jay Novocek was nonetheless one of Aikman's favorite targets. He scored Dallas's first points in both Super Bowl XXVII and Super Bowl XXX on touchdown passes from Aikman. In fact, if you had to name an all-time Super Bowl team, Novocek, with his three rings and seventeen total receptions, deserves consideration at tight end.

You Again?

Some players have a habit of getting back to the Super Bowl no matter which team they happen to play for. Here are some of the players we've seen quite a bit on Super Sunday.

1. MIKE LODISH

Mike Lodish has taken the field on Super Sunday more times than any player; he's been in six games. He first played in Super Bowl XXV as a reserve offensive lineman with the Buffalo Bills. He stayed with the Bills through their four consecutive Super Bowls before leaving to join the Denver Broncos. Still a reserve, he made his final two appearances in Super Bowls XXXII (in which he won his first ring) and XXXIII.

2. CHARLES HALEY

The charismatic defensive end for the 49ers and the Cowboys, Charles Haley holds the record for the most Super Bowl victories: five. His five-for-five stretch began as a 49er with Super Bowl XXIII versus the Bengals and ended as a Cowboy with Super Bowl XXX against the Steelers. In between he played on two of the biggest blowouts in Super Bowl history: San Francisco's 55–10 win over Denver in Super Bowl XXIV and Dallas's 52–17 demolition of Buffalo in Super Bowl XXVII.

3.   MARV FLEMING

Tight end Marv Fleming was with Vince Lombardi's Packers in Super Bowls I and II. Five years later, as a member of the Miami Dolphins, he became the first player to win Super Bowls with two different franchises. For his career, Fleming played in five Super Bowls (I and II with Green Bay; VI, VII, and VIII with Miami) and was victorious in four of the five.

4.   KEN NORTON

Ken Norton has the distinction of being the only player to win three consecutive Super Bowl rings. The son of the former heavyweight boxing champion, Norton started at linebacker for the Cowboys in Super Bowls XXVII and XXVIII, even scoring a touchdown on a fumble return in his first appearance. But following the 1993 season, he left Dallas to sign as a free agent with the San Francisco 49ers. In his first year by the bay, the 49ers stormed to the Super Bowl, defeating Dallas along the way in the NFC Championship Game. In Miami's Joe Robbie Stadium, Norton took home his third ring when the 49ers walloped the San Diego Chargers, 49–26.

5.   PRESTON PEARSON

Running back Preston Pearson was the first player to compete in Super Bowls for three different franchises, and also the first to play with one franchise in one game, then play against that same franchise the next year. Pearson's first exposure to the big game was in his third season, when his Baltimore Colts advanced to Super Bowl III and were knocked off by the Jets, 16–7. He had a couple of kickoff returns in that game. A few years later he joined the Pittsburgh Steelers and was there for their first championship in Super Bowl IX. But being a running back on a squad with Franco Harris and Rocky Bleier meant limited offensive playing time. The following year with Dallas, he saw more action on the offensive side of the ball in addition to his special teams work and got to play against his former team in Super Bowl X. Pearson had 67 yards of total offense in that game. He stayed with the Cowboys through two more Super Bowl appearances, making valuable contributions in each game.

6. BILL ROMANOWSKI

Love him or hate him—and most hate him—linebacker Bill Romanowski had a knack for finding teams to take him to the Super Bowl. Romanowski is one of the few who have played for three different teams in the big game, and along with Gene Upshaw, he is one of only two men to play in the Super Bowl in three different decades. Romo's first Super Bowl was XXIII, when as a rookie, he was part of the 49ers defense that held the high-powered Bengals' offense without an offensive touchdown. He also tipped the ball to himself on a spectacular interception of Boomer Esiason. Romanowski was back the following year to win his second straight Super Bowl, and then eight years later he returned with the Denver Broncos. In Super Bowl XXXII John Elway got his first ring, while Romanowski picked up his third. He won his fourth the following year. In 2002 the fifteen-year veteran helped lead the Raiders to Super Bowl XXXVII, but his effort to tie Charles Haley with the most Super Bowl rings was thwarted by the Tampa Bay Buccaneers, 48–21.

7. DON BEEBE

Don Beebe won the hearts of America with his hustle play against Leon Lett in Super Bowl XXVII. Beebe was on the roster for all four of the Bills' Super Bowl losses (although he missed Super Bowl XXV with an injury). For all his heartbreak, the football gods rewarded him just three seasons following his final Super Bowl with the Bills. The Green Bay Packers picked him up as a dependable veteran to put on the field in multiple wide receiver formations, and the Packers went on to Super Bowl XXXI. When Green Bay clinched their 35–21 victory, quarterback Brett Favre handed the game ball to Beebe. Beebe became the first player from the Bills' Super Bowl–losing teams to win a ring.

8. CORNELIUS BENNETT

Like Beebe, Bennett was part of the Bills' run to four consecutive Super Bowl appearances. Also like Beebe, he made it back to the big game later in his career. But unlike Beebe, his fifth trip to the Super Bowl ended just like the first four. Bennett was brought in to the Atlanta Falcons as a veteran leader at the linebacker spot and made it to Super Bowl XXXIII when Atlanta upset Minnesota in the NFC Championship Game. But when the Falcons met the Broncos, Bennett left with a fifth Super Bowl loss.

9. GALE GILBERT

Backup quarterback Gale Gilbert was with the Buffalo Bills from 1990 through 1993 and with the San Diego Chargers in 1994. So he was on teams that went to five consecutive Super Bowls. The only problem? His team lost all five games.

10. THE 1970S DALLAS COWBOYS

The Cowboys had five players who played in Super Bowls V, VI, X, XII, and XIII: defensive end Larry Cole, safeties Charlie Waters and Cliff Harris, linebacker D. D. Lewis, and offensive tackle Rayfield Wright.

They Never Played in the Super Bowl?

A player regrets nothing more when his career has come to an end than not having won a championship. There are a number of great NFL players, many who are enshrined in the Hall of Fame, who never had the opportunity to play in the big game. Some hit bad luck; some didn't have the supporting cast. Here are some of the best-known players who never made it to the Super Bowl.

1. DICK BUTKUS

Dick Butkus patrolled the middle of the Chicago Bears' defense from 1965 through 1974 and became one of the most feared defenders in NFL history. But Butkus never played in a playoff game, never mind a Super Bowl. Butkus's Bears had a few problems: They never had a great quarterback, and they played in the same division as first, the Lombardi Packers, and later, the Bud Grant Vikings. One of the strangest facts in NFL history is that the 1969 Bears finished 1–13, even though they had both Butkus and Gale Sayers.

2. O. J. SIMPSON

For most of his career, O. J. Simpson was a one-man show. Behind a strong offensive line, O. J. became the only running back to rush for more than 2,000 yards in a fourteen-game season in 1973. But his teams made the playoffs only once, in 1974 when the Bills traveled to Pittsburgh and were trounced by the Steelers, 32–14. He finished his career in 1979 on a dreadful 49ers team. Two seasons later, the Niners won their first of five Super Bowls.

3. EARL CAMPBELL

Earl Campbell came out of the University of Texas in 1978 and joined Bum Phillips's Houston Oilers. His presence in the backfield immediately transformed the Oilers from a pretty good team to a squad with a legitimate chance to overthrow the Steelers as the best in the AFC. In Campbell's rookie year the Oilers made it to the AFC Championship Game in Pittsburgh, but lost. The next year the Oilers followed the same script. Despite Coach Phillips's boast that after "hammering on the door . . . next season we're going to kick the sumbitch in," Campbell never won another playoff game.

4. DAN FOUTS

The field general behind the Chargers' Air Coryell offense in the 1970s and 1980s, Dan Fouts threw for more than 43,000 yards and 254 touchdowns in a fifteen-year Hall of Fame career. He and his Chargers had three very good opportunities to reach the Super Bowl, but each time, they walked away with bitter disappointment. In 1979 the Chargers won the AFC West and trounced both the Steelers and Rams (the two eventual Super Bowl teams) during the regular season, but they were upset at home by the wild-card Oilers, 17–14 in the divisional playoff. The following year they again won the division but were knocked off by the Oakland Raiders in the AFC Championship Game in San Diego. Then in 1981 the Chargers went on the road for the AFC title game and lost in the frigid cold to the Cincinnati Bengals, 27–7. That loss was Fouts's last shot at making it to the big game.

5. STEVE LARGENT

Wide receiver Steve Largent enjoyed a long, record-breaking career in relative anonymity in Seattle. A dependable target for quarterbacks Jim Zorn and, later, Dave Krieg, Largent was at his best on third down. Largent had only one really good chance to make the Super Bowl, and that came in 1983. After a 9–7 regular season, the Seahawks knocked off the Broncos in the wild-card game and then upset the Dolphins and rookie quarterback Dan Marino in the Orange Bowl to advance to the AFC Championship Game. There they faced the Raiders at the Los Angeles Coliseum, and although the Seahawks had beaten the Raiders twice during the regular season, the Silver and Black prevailed, 30–14. Largent retired with a then-NFL record of 819 career receptions and 177 consecutive games with a reception.

6. BARRY SANDERS

Barry Sanders may have been the best running back ever at making something out of nothing. Countless times, he looked to be trapped by defenders in the backfield, only to break free on a long gain. His stats for his ten-year career are remarkable: more than 15,000 yards rushing, an average of 5 yards per carry, and a remarkable 2,053 yards in 1997. But he spent his entire career with the Detroit Lions. Now think about it: How many great Lions can you name who played with Sanders? Herman Moore, perhaps. He had a few great years at wide receiver for Detroit. But that's it. The Lions were always better than average but never great. That's why they won only one playoff game in Sanders's career.

7.   ARCHIE MANNING

Archie Manning played for so many bad teams, it's easy to forget that he was widely regarded as one of the most talented quarterbacks in the league for more than a decade. A superstar out of Ole Miss, Manning stayed in the South as a pro, with the New Orleans Saints. Saints' fans hoped that Manning would lead their team to the promised land, but New Orleans management was unable to provide him with a supporting cast. Manning, in a fourteen-year career (He mopped up his last few years with Houston and Minnesota.) never got to play in the postseason.

8.   ROMAN GABRIEL

Roman Gabriel was one of the premier NFL quarterbacks in the 1960s and 1970s, playing for one of its premier teams, the Los Angeles Rams. From 1967 through 1970, Gabriel led the Rams to forty-one wins against eleven losses and four ties, but the Rams made the playoffs only twice in those years. Gabriel's best chance to reach the Super Bowl was in 1967. The Rams finished 11–1–2, but because of an old NFL rule, the playoff home field was determined on a rotating basis and was not decided by record. So Los Angeles had to travel to 9–4–1 Green Bay for their first-round playoff game. As you might expect, the warm-weather Rams had a difficult time with the Pack, losing 28–7.

9. KELLEN WINSLOW

See Dan Fouts, above. A teammate of Fouts with the San Diego Chargers, Kellen Winslow led the NFL in receptions twice and in two other seasons finished second and third, respectively. The five-time Pro-Bowler is best remembered for his performance in the Chargers classic 41–38 overtime win over the Dolphins in the 1981 divisional playoffs. In that game he had thirteen catches for 166 yards and a touchdown, and he blocked an Uwe von Schamann field goal attempt to keep San Diego in the game.

10. TROY VINCENT

Through the 2003 regular season, twelve-year veteran Troy Vincent has played on a number of playoff teams with the Miami Dolphins and Philadelphia Eagles. But he's never reached the promised land, despite coming close for three straight years. The Eagles lost consecutive NFC Championship Games to the Rams in St. Louis in 2001 and then at home to Tampa Bay and Carolina in 2002 and 2003.

We Could Have Been Contenders!

As great an event as the Super Bowl is, the best teams throughout the season don't always wind up there: Some teams are upset in the playoffs, some are hit by the injury bug at the wrong time, some run into bad luck, but once the Super Bowl comes around, all the good things these team have accomplished from September through December are forgotten. Here are ten of the best teams who watched the Super Bowl from their living rooms.

1. 1990 SAN FRANCISCO 49ERS

The 49ers were on their way to becoming the first team to win three straight Super Bowls. They started the season 10–0 and wound up 14–2. Joe Montana threw for almost 4,000 yards, with 1,500 of those yards going to Jerry Rice. Their defense was steady all year, giving up more than three touchdowns just twice. In the playoffs they dismantled the Redskins before running into the New York Giants in the NFC

Jon SooHoo

Joe Montana had four Super Bowl rings from the eighties,
but could have won a fifth in 1990. The 14–2 Niners—and
Montana personally—were knocked out of the
NFC Championship Game by the Giants.

Championship Game at Candlestick Park. Like the 49ers, the Giants started the season 10–0 but lost a memorable Monday night game at the Stick in December. In the NFC championship New York took advantage of a Montana injury (caused by a vicious hit from Leonard Marshall), a big gain by Gary Reasons on a fake punt, a late Roger Craig fumble, and five Matt Bahr field goals to knock off the 49ers, 15–13. The Giants then beat the Bills in Super Bowl XXV.

2. 1975 MINNESOTA VIKINGS

Yes, the Vikings did go to four Super Bowls in eight seasons, but many Vikings watchers feel that they may have fielded their best all-around team in 1975. Fran Tarkenton threw for twenty-five touchdowns, and Chuck Foreman ran for 1,070 yards. They started the season 10–0 before losses to Washington and Detroit in their final four games. With the exception of the Redskins game, the Minnesota defense was dominant all season, giving up twenty points or more just twice, and their dominance continued into their divisional playoff game against Dallas at Metropolitan Stadium, as they held the Cowboys to just ten points through the first fifty-eight minutes. But Dallas quarterback Roger Staubach had a little magic left, hitting wide receiver Drew Pearson with a 50-yard bomb to win the game. To this day, the Vikings and their fans are convinced that offensive pass interference should have been called against Pearson, but the flag never came.

3. 1998 MINNESOTA VIKINGS

It was a new generation of Vikings, but 1998 may have had a more disappointing ending for Minnesotans than 1975. In '98 the Vikings became just the third team in

NFL history to finish a season with a 15–1 record, set a league record by scoring 556 points behind quarterback Randall Cunningham and rookie receiver Randy Moss, and sent nine players to the Pro Bowl. The Atlanta Falcons came to the Metrodome for the NFC Championship Game as a big underdog, and they trailed the Vikings by a touchdown late in the fourth quarter until everything went wrong for the Vikings. Gary Anderson, who had not missed a kick all season, missed a 38-yard field goal, and the Falcons scored a late touchdown to force overtime. The Vikings failed to score in the extra session, Cunningham missed an open Moss on a long pass play, and the Falcons advanced to the Super Bowl on a Morten Andersen field goal.

4. 1976 PITTSBURGH STEELERS

In 1976 the Steelers were coming off back-to-back Super Bowl championships but stumbled out of the gate, losing four of their first five games. But they turned their season around with probably the most dominant nine-game defensive stretch in NFL history. Pittsburgh won their final nine games, during which they had five shutouts and relinquished only twenty-eight total points. That's twenty-eight points in nine games—and sixteen of those came in a single game against Houston. The Steelers finished 10–4 and won the AFC Central. Then they trounced the Colts in Baltimore to advance to the AFC Championship Game. But that game proved costly—both of the Steelers' star running backs, Franco Harris and Rocky Bleier, were injured. So Pittsburgh went to Oakland with a depleted offense and were knocked off by the Raiders, 24–7.

5. 1996 DENVER BRONCOS

It seemed like 1996 would be Denver quarterback John Elway's best chance to bring home a Super Bowl championship. Running back Terrell Davis gave the offense a dimension that Elway's offenses had not had before. The Broncos wound up with a record of 13–3 and had home-field advantage throughout the AFC playoffs. But in a remarkable upset, the second-year Jacksonville Jaguars, led by quarterback Mark Brunell, stormed into Mile High Stadium and pulled off a 30–27 win.

6. 1987 SAN FRANCISCO 49ERS

The 49ers finished the strike-marred 1987 season with the best record in the NFL at 13–2 and won their final three regular season games by a combined score of 124–7. (Read that last sentence again; it's not a misprint.) All their offensive stars were big contributors, from Joe Montana to Jerry Rice to Roger Craig, and the defense was really coming into its own during a season-ending six-game winning streak. But all this fell apart in one game—a divisional playoff loss to the Vikings at Candlestick Park. The final score was 36–24, but it wasn't that close. The 49ers were embarrassed, trailing by as many as seventeen points, and Montana was benched for Steve Young. San Francisco got their revenge in the following year's playoffs, when they beat Minnesota on their way to another Super Bowl championship.

7. 1967 LOS ANGELES RAMS

The Rams were, to be blunt, screwed by the NFL's playoff format. Because the league alternated which division champion had the home field each year, the team with the best record did not always host the game. Such was the case with the Rams, who finished 11–1–2 but had to go on the road to play the 9–4–1 defending NFL champion Green Bay Packers. The Packers lost to the Rams during the regular season, but in the postseason the Packers had never lost a home game. That streak continued in the playoff game, as the Packers, in a frigid afternoon at Milwaukee's County Stadium, trounced the Rams, 28–7.

8.   1967 BALTIMORE COLTS

This team might be the best never to make the playoffs. They had the misfortune to play in the same division as the Rams (see above entry) and finished with an identical 11–1–2 record. But in those days, the NFL did not have a wild-card team, so three teams who failed to win more than nine games advanced to the playoffs, and the 11-win Colts (who lost the tiebreaker to the Rams by finishing 0–1–1 against them) stayed home. Think about the Colts for a second. They followed this season up with what is widely considered one of the best regular seasons ever, when they finished 13–1 in 1968 before losing Super Bowl III to the Jets. So Baltimore went two seasons with a record of 24–2–2 but didn't have a championship ring to show for their troubles.

9.   1969 OAKLAND RAIDERS

The Raiders were dominant for a third consecutive regular season, finishing 12–1–1 and winning the AFC Western division. But 1969 was the first year that the AFL experimented with wild-card playoff entries (although they were not called that at the time). They trounced the East wild-card Houston, 40–7, and then faced the West wild-card Kansas City in the championship game. The Raiders had beaten the Chiefs twice during the regular season but were defeated 17–7 at the Oakland Coliseum, one in a series of bitter playoff losses the team suffered from 1968 through 1977. In the Raiders' three-year stretch from 1967 until 1969, they went 37–4–1 in the regular season but 2–3 in the postseason.

10. **1975 LOS ANGELES RAMS**

Another in a long line of disappointments for the Rams in the 1970s, the 1975 season may have been their most disheartening. They finished 12–2 and won the NFC West. During the regular season, their defense, led by Jack and Jim Youngblood, Jack Reynolds, and Bill Simpson, allowed just 135 points (fewer than ten per game), and opponents scored more than twenty just once. But in the NFC Championship Game at the L.A. Coliseum, the Rams were embarrassed by the Dallas Cowboys (see #2 above). Dallas, who received great games from quarterback Roger Staubach and running back Preston Pearson, destroyed Los Angeles 37–7.

The Silver and Black

The Oakland Raiders are the NFL's version of the schoolyard punk. They're always doing and saying things that make you uncomfortable, they look menacing, and you never want to get on their bad side. That's the image franchise owner Al Davis has cultivated, and it's brought three championships to Oakland and Los Angeles. See that, even when switching schools, they're still a bully.

1. GENE UPSHAW AND ART SHELL

Gene Upshaw and Art Shell were the anchors of the Oakland offensive line in the 1970s, as the left guard and tackle. The Hall of Famers were at their best in Super Bowl XI, when they led the charge against the Vikings defense, on the way to 266 yards rushing. They each won a second ring four years later as the Raiders took Super Bowl XV from the Eagles. More significant is what the two accomplished off the field after retirement. Upshaw has long been an executive with the NFL players' union, and in 1989 Shell became the first African-American head coach in NFL history when he replaced Mike Shanahan as coach of the, you guessed it, Raiders.

2. FRED BILETNIKOFF

Fred Biletnikoff always seemed to have a dirty jersey. He also had stickum all over his hands, long dirty-blond hair, and an unkempt mustache. He looked like he should have been changing oil at a service center outside the Oakland Alameda County Coliseum, rather than catching passes inside. But despite appearances, Biletnikoff was a leading receiver for the Raiders for fourteen seasons. He was one of four Raiders who lost to the Packers in Super Bowl II who were still on the team for their Super Bowl XI win over the Vikings. Biletnikoff was the MVP in the January 1977 game with four catches, three of which set up his team inside the 5-yard line.

3. JACK TATUM

A vicious safety out of Ohio State, he personified the Raiders' meanness. Heck, the guy's nickname was "The Assassin." That ought to give you an idea of how Tatum hit. He manned the secondary for the Raiders for a long time but appeared in only one big game, their win in Super Bowl XI. And boy, did he ever make his presence known in that one. Ask Sammie White, the Vikings' rookie wide receiver. He took a shot from Tatum that knocked White one direction, his helmet another, and his chinstrap in yet another.

4. JIM PLUNKETT

How do you go from Heisman Trophy finalist and first-round draft pick to journeyman in a decade? And how do you then turn it all around to become a two-time Super Bowl–winning quarterback? With a lot of perseverance, Jim Plunkett did just that. But it took an injury to new Raiders quarterback Dan Pastorini early in the 1980 season for Plunkett to get his shot. He led the Raiders to the wild card in the AFC and then won three playoff games before knocking off the Eagles in Super Bowl XV. Then for good measure, he stuck around three more years to guide the Raiders to their surprisingly easy Super Bowl XVIII win over the Redskins.

5. TOM FLORES

Normally, when a coach wins two Super Bowls, fans and media want to place him on a coaching pedestal. This was not the case with Tom Flores, who guided the Raiders to wins in Super Bowls XV and XVIII. Perhaps that's because he emerged from the shadow cast by John Madden, whom he replaced, or maybe because the specter of Davis continued to loom in Raiders' coaching legacy. But Flores never seemed to get the respect that other coaches with two Super Bowl wins received. (Mike Shanahan comes to mind.) Perhaps more interesting is that Flores came to the Raiders as a coach after spending part of his playing career with the hated Chiefs! He even backed up Lenny Dawson at quarterback in Super Bowl IV.

6. LESTER HAYES

Here is another Raider who made the most out of stickum before the NFL outlawed it. In the Raiders' Super Bowl season of 1980, cornerback Lester Hayes challenged Dick "Night Train" Lane's all-time single season interception record when he finished with thirteen. He was also instrumental in shutting down the Redskins' potent passing game in Super Bowl XVIII. Oh, and his nickname was "the Molester." Get it? Lester the Molester. First the Assassin, then the Molester. The lesson here is don't let your daughter grow up to date Raiders' defensive backs.

7. RAY GUY

It has to be an awful lot of pressure to be a first-round draft pick. Now imagine that you're both a first-round draft pick and a punter. Ray Guy faced that, but he lived up to all expectations and more, winning three Super Bowl rings with the Raiders.

8. LYLE ALZADO

Lyle Alzado was another grizzled veteran that most teams felt was beyond his prime. But the Raiders brought the ex-Bronco and ex-Brown in, and once installed on their defensive line, he helped win Super Bowl XVIII. Tragically, it came to light after his retirement that he had abused steroids as a player. He later died of brain cancer.

9. CLIFF BRANCH

Another guy who seemed to play for the Raiders for about thirty-five years, fleet wide receiver Cliff Branch actually played fourteen seasons with the Silver and Black. Branch was on the victorious squads in Super Bowls XI, XV, and XVIII and accounted for fourteen catches for 181 yards and three touchdowns.

10. **MARCUS ALLEN**

Marcus Allen played in only one big game for the Raiders, but he owned the Redskins' defense in Super Bowl XVIII, rushing for 191 yards. His 74-yard touchdown on a cutback in the second half was a thing of beauty, and it easily earned him the game's MVP Award.

Head Scratchers

Coaches work their whole lives to get to the Super Bowl. Some leave having achieved their ultimate goal, but the losing coach must go home with what-ifs sticking in his craw for the entire off-season. "Is there anything I would have done differently?" the losing coaches wonder. A few other coaches, though, made extremely questionable calls in their Super Bowl appearances, and not surprisingly, most of them went home with a loss.

1. JOE GIBBS

The play remains etched in the minds of Redskins fans everywhere. Down 14–3 to the Raiders, inside their own 20-yard line, with twelve seconds left in the first half of Super Bowl XVIII, Joe Gibbs's quarterback, Joe Theismann, had a screen pass picked off by Raiders linebacker Jack Squirek for a touchdown. Why didn't Gibbs just sit on the ball, content to go into the second half down eleven points?

Earlier in the season, the two teams met in RFK Stadium. Late in the first half of that game, Gibbs called the same play, and running back Joe Washington scampered for a 67-yard gain that put the Redskins in position to score. But how could Gibbs call that play again, against the same team, just a few months later? The Raiders were waiting for it. The Redskins took the opening kickoff of the second half down the field for a touchdown, and had that score made it a five-point game as opposed to a twelve-point game, the outcome may have been different.

2. MARV LEVY

Late in the first half of Super Bowl XXVIII, the Bills led the Cowboys, 10–6, and were driving deep in Dallas territory. They had a first down at the Dallas 12, and they were set to receive the second-half kickoff, putting them firmly in the driver's seat. But Marv Levy became a little conservative with his play calling. The Bills threw the ball three times, but not one pass went into the end zone, and they settled for a Steve Christie field goal. They took a seven point lead into the half, but their tentativeness late in the half came back to haunt them on the third play of the third quarter. That's when Dallas safety James Washington scooped up a Thurman Thomas fumble and scampered 46 yards for a touchdown. The Bills did not score again, and the Cowboys won their second consecutive Super Bowl.

3. DON SHULA

Here's a dilemma for you: When your offense is struggling to score points in the Super Bowl, do you replace your league-MVP quarterback with a quarterback who is widely regarded as the best to ever play the position? That's a decision Don Shula faced in Super Bowl III. Earl Morrall replaced the injured Johnny Unitas in the 1968 season and led the Colts to a 13–1 record, earning NFL MVP honors. But in Super Bowl III, Unitas was waiting on the bench, watching Morrall go just six for seventeen for 71 yards. He was also picked off three times. It was not until just over three minutes remained in the third quarter, with the Colts trailing 13–0, that Unitas got the call to enter the game. He led the Colts to a fourth-quarter touchdown, but it was too little, too late, as Joe Namath and the Jets pulled off the 16–7 upset. Shula was left to answer questions as to why he left Morrall in as long as he did.

4. CHUCK NOLL

You won't find many coaches on this list whose teams actually won the game. In fact, you'll find just one: Chuck Noll. He's here for opting not to punt late in the fourth quarter of Super Bowl X. His Steelers led the Cowboys, 21–17, with a little under two minutes remaining, and they faced a fourth-and-nine on the Dallas 41-yard line. Quarterback Terry Bradshaw had earlier been knocked out of the game, so Terry Hanratty was calling the signals. Noll wanted to avoid a blocked punt, and reasoning that the Cowboys had no timeouts remaining, called a running play. Running back Rocky Bleier was stopped for a two-yard gain. The decision looked extremely questionable after two Dallas plays moved the ball to the Pittsburgh 38-yard line. The Cowboys didn't score, thanks to Glen Edwards' end-zone interception, but Noll became one of the few coaches to be second-guessed in a Super Bowl that he won!

5. DICK VERMEIL

Are decisions made by a coach in the week leading up to the game just as important as the decisions he makes on the sidelines on Super Bowl Sunday? In the days leading up to Super Bowl XV in New Orleans, Dick Vermeil kept a tight leash on his Philadelphia Eagles, treating the big game as a high-pressure business trip. Their opponents, however, the Oakland Raiders, were frequent visitors to Bourbon Street and much more relaxed heading into the game. The Eagles looked and played tight. They certainly did not resemble the team that had dismantled the Dallas Cowboys in the NFC Championship Game just two weeks earlier. The Raiders made the game look easy, a 27–10 romp, and many made the point in the postgame that the Eagles' tightness during the game could have been a result of their regimented week.

6. BILL CALLAHAN

The Oakland Raiders stormed to the AFC championship under first-year head coach Bill Callahan. In Super Bowl XXXVII they went up against a familiar opponent: former head coach Jon Gruden, who led the Tampa Bay Buccaneers to the Super Bowl in his first year with the team. Although the Raiders were heavily favored to win, the Buccaneers coasted to a rather easy victory. Why? Well, the Tampa defense claimed they recognized all of Oakland's formations because they were the same formations run when Gruden was coaching the Raiders! How on earth could Callahan not change things up for the Super Bowl?

7. MIKE MARTZ

Mike Martz took enough heat when the Patriots in Super Bowl XXXVI defeated his heavily favored Rams, and the primary focus of the complaints was his use of all-world running back Marshall Faulk. Faulk, who was widely regarded as the best back in the league during the season, got only twenty-one touches against the vaunted New England defense, and he rushed for only 76 yards. The Rams were held to just seventeen points and seemingly kept their most dangerous offensive weapon in the holster.

8. **JEFF FISHER**

The Tennessee Titans had done very little in three quarters. They trailed the St. Louis Rams 16–0 in Super Bowl XXXIV, before finally breaking through for an Eddie George touchdown just seconds before the start of the fourth quarter. Since the Titans had no success stopping the Rams from moving into scoring position throughout the game, Titans coach Jeff Fisher decided to go for the two-point conversion, thinking that two points would get him within a touchdown and another two-point conversion of a tie. The conversion attempt was no good, but the Titans managed a field goal and a touchdown to tie the game in the fourth quarter. In hindsight, going for the single extra point would have given them seven points, and the ten they added in the fourth quarter would have given them the lead.

9. **JIM FASSEL**

The Giants trailed the Ravens, 10–0, late in the second quarter of Super Bowl XXXV, and their offense was finally making some headway against the vaunted Ravens defense. With the ball at the Baltimore 29-yard line, the Giants had a little over a minute until halftime and desperately needed to put points on the board. But instead of playing it safe and getting a score, the

Giants were greedy. On first down, New York quarter-back Kerry Collins, who had not been sharp all day, lofted an ill-advised pass into double coverage in the end zone. Ravens cornerback Chris McAlister came up with an interception, and the Giants' offense squandered their best scoring opportunity in the game.

10.   JOHN FOX

With his Carolina Panthers trailing the New England Patriots early in the fourth quarter of Super Bowl XXXVIII, Fox faced a decision. Carolina scored a touchdown to cut New England's lead to 21–16, pending the extra point. Fox opted to go for the two-point conversion to bring his team within a field goal of the Patriots. It seemed early to be going for two, and it looked worse when they were unable to convert. The first missed conversion forced Carolina to go for two again after their next touchdown gave them a 22–21 lead. They failed to convert on that one as well. The Panthers left a couple of points on the board, which made a huge difference at the end of the game. Had Carolina gone for extra points instead of conversions, Adam Vinatieri's field goal attempt would have been to tie, rather than win, the game.

Run to Daylight

The old adage in the NFL is that if you want to win, you've got to be able to run the ball, and you have to be able to stop the run. The Super Bowl has demonstrated time and again the value of a strong running game. From Elijah Pitts to Michael Pittman, running backs are often the difference between winning the trophy and going home empty-handed.

1. EMMITT SMITH

Emmitt Smith was the vital cog in the Cowboys' three Super Bowl championships in the 1990s. He carried the ball seventy times in those games, and scored five touchdowns on the ground (a Super Bowl record). His biggest moments came late, as he scored two second-half touchdowns in Dallas's 30–13 win over the Bills in Super Bowl XXVIII and ran in another two in their 27–17 win over the Steelers in Super Bowl XXX.

Jon SooHoo

Emmitt Smith, the heart and soul of three
Dallas Cowboys Super Bowl Championship teams.

2. **FRANCO HARRIS**

Before the Steelers could win four Super Bowl titles in the 1970s, they needed to win their first. Everyone in the Steel City should thank Franco Harris for getting the ball rolling (or rushing, as it were). In Super Bowl IX Franco punished the Vikings' defense, galloping for 158 yards (then a Super Bowl record). His numbers in Super Bowl XIII and XIV were not as impressive, but in each game, he scored a pivotal touchdown to put a win out of reach for his opponents. He finished his four Super Bowls with 354 total yards rushing, a record.

3. **ELIJAH PITTS**

Paul Hornung was hurt and unable to play, so the Packers had to rely on two backs in Super Bowl I: veteran Jim Taylor and Elijah Pitts. Pitts's numbers were modest: eleven rushes for 45 yards, but he did become the first of many backs to rush for two touchdowns in a Super Bowl game.

4. **LARRY CSONKA**

Larry Csonka may have been the most recognizable Dolphin on the Miami team that went to three straight Super Bowls with his trademark facemask, tough-guy beard, and body of a bull. Csonka also may have been the most important player for Miami in their two Super Bowl wins. Against Washington in Super Bowl VII, he ran for 112 yards on only fifteen carries, including a battering 49-yard jaunt in the second half. The following year against Minnesota, he destroyed the Vikings' defense, rushing for 145 yards on thirty-three carries, with two touchdowns. For his Super Bowl career, he averaged 5.2 yards per carry.

5. JOHN RIGGINS

He was one of the great characters of the game—just look at how many different hair styles the guy had! But John Riggins was more than just hair. At his best, he could be one of the most dominant backs in the game. Thanks to him, the Redskins defeated the Dolphins in Super Bowl XVII. His 43-yard touchdown run in the fourth quarter on a fourth-and-one play gave the Redskins the lead for good, and he ran over the Killer Bees defense for 166 yards total.

6. TERRELL DAVIS

John Elway had played for fourteen years and had not won a Super Bowl. He also played most of those years without any kind of dependable running game. But then in 1995, the Broncos drafted Terrell Davis out of the University of Georgia. It's no coincidence, then, that the Broncos put together one of the greatest three-season runs in NFL history, a 46–10 record (including postseason) and two Super Bowl titles, once Davis joined the team. Elway and Davis teamed up to lead the Broncos in their first Super Bowl, as Davis recovered from a second-quarter migraine to rush for 157 yards and three touchdowns (including the game-winner) in their 31–24 win over the Packers in Super Bowl XXXII. He added 102 yards the next year in Denver's win over the Atlanta Falcons.

7. OTTIS ANDERSON

Ottis Anderson was in his eighth season with the Cardinals when he was sent to the New York Giants. Many thought the trade signaled the end of the line for Ottis, but the move to New York rejuvenated him. He scored a late touchdown in Super Bowl XXI, in the Giants' win over the Broncos, and four years later, he was still going strong. He capped his marvelous career when the Giants took on the Bills in Super Bowl XXV. Ottis's 102 yards and a pivotal third-quarter touchdown earned him the game's MVP.

8. DUANE THOMAS

He was an enigma to many, even his teammates in Dallas. He once responded to a reporter who questioned him about an upcoming Super Bowl, "If this is the ultimate game, then why are they playing it again next year?" Duane Thomas should be thankful they play the game once a year because he was able to use his second appearance to atone for a pivotal fumble in his first, Super Bowl V against the Colts. In the Cowboys' Super Bowl VI win over the Miami Dolphins, Thomas galloped for 95 yards and a touchdown. Dallas won their first world championship, 24–3.

9. TONY DORSETT

You can't have a better two years than Tony Dorsett had in 1976 and 1977. When the Heisman Trophy winner was a senior at Pitt in 1976, the Panthers went undefeated and won the national championship. In 1977 the Dallas Cowboys drafted him, and he fit right in with a veteran team, leading Dallas to a 12–2 record and a Super Bowl championship over Denver. He ran for 66 yards and a touchdown. Then the following year, Dorsett again led the Cowboys to the Super Bowl, rushing for 96 yards, but his numbers weren't enough; Tony's magic ran out, and the Steelers beat the Cowboys, 35–31.

10. EDDIE GEORGE

Eddie George couldn't run his Titans to a Super Bowl XXXIV win over the St. Louis Rams, but his efforts kept them close, and gave them a fighting chance on their final drive. George, the Heisman winner from Ohio State, rushed for 95 yards and two second-half touchdowns. More than 70 of his yards came after intermission as the Titans furiously rallied from sixteen points down to tie the score before the Rams eventually won, 23–16.

Saving Their Worst for Last

From 1969 through 1976 Bud Grant's Minnesota Vikings had an overall regular season record of 87–24–1, a .781 winning percentage, and an NFC playoff record of 8–3, which is a winning percentage of .727. During that eight-year span, they won seven NFL or NFC Central championships. Four times they won twelve games in a season; twice they won eleven. Four times the Vikings won the NFC championship and advanced to the Super Bowl. Each time, their counterparts from the AFL or AFC soundly defeated them. How did it happen? How did a team whose regular season exploits matched those of the Dallas Cowboys and Pittsburgh Steelers from the same era always come up empty in the Super Bowl?

1. THE PURPLE PEOPLE EATERS

Carl Eller, Jim Marshall, Alan Page, Gary Larsen, and later Doug Sutherland formed one of the most feared front fours in NFL history. Their pressure consistently made the Vikings one of the best defenses in the league against the pass, but in their four Super Bowl appearances, the Purple People Eaters were a bust. Each of their opponents seemingly moved the ball at will against them, particularly on the ground. Look at the numbers: In Super Bowl IV the Chiefs gained 151 yards on the ground; in Super Bowl VIII Miami rushed for 196; Pittsburgh had a remarkable 249 in Super Bowl IX; and finally Oakland ran for 266 (!) in Super Bowl XI.

2. FRAN TARKENTON

The undersized Tarkenton gave the Vikings the mobility that most drop-back quarterbacks did not possess. His scrambling enabled his receivers to find spots in the downfield coverage, and Tark always made the defense pay if they gave him that extra bit of time. But in Tarkenton's three Super Bowls with Minnesota, he failed to unleash any of his magic. He led the team to just two offensive touchdowns in those games and had only one touchdown pass.

3. WHERE'S THE OFFENSE?

In addition to Tarkenton's struggles, it should be noted that the rest of the offense had their own problems. The Vikings were forced to punt twenty-one times in their four games, and their running game was almost nonexistent. Their leading rusher in Super Bowl IV was Bill Brown with 26 yards; in Super Bowl VIII it was Oscar Reed with 32; Super Bowl IX it was Chuck Foreman, with a whopping 18 yards; and in Super Bowl XI Foreman again led the way with 44 yards. Now compare those numbers with those of their opponents, and there's little wonder who the winning teams were.

4. BUD GRANT

Bud Grant had quite a career even *before* he coached the Vikings. He was a collegiate star in both basketball and football and played on the 1950 NBA champion Minneapolis Lakers. Later, he won three Grey Cups as a head coach in the Canadian Football League. He was as much the symbol of his Viking teams as any of his players, and all in his organization loved him. He's enshrined in the Pro Football Hall of Fame, and he richly deserves it. But he clearly had some of his worst days on Super Bowl Sundays. He rarely found an adjustment that worked. If an opponent took the lead, he had no answer; perhaps most tellingly, his teams never led in any of the four games.

5. REGULAR SEASON DOMINANCE

The numbers above are a testament to the strength of the Vikings from September through December. No one ever wanted to play the Vikings, especially in Metropolitan Stadium. In their seven division-winning seasons, the closest another team finished to them was two games in 1970. In 1973 Minnesota won the division by five and a half games, and it was only a fourteen-game season! It surely made things easier that the team could start preparing for the postseason at about the time Halloween came.

6. THE MET

Metropolitan Stadium, in Bloomington, Minnesota, was a dump. A minor league baseball stadium, it was expanded to become the home of the Twins baseball team and the Vikings. Its football capacity was under 50,000, its odd configuration forced both teams to stand on the same sideline, and its fans were among the most boisterous in the league. And that's not to mention the weather. Bitter cold came into play in just about any game played after October 15, giving the Vikings one of the most pronounced home-field advantages in the whole league. You can bet that the Vikings and their fans believe the Super Bowls would have had different outcomes had those teams had to travel up to Minnesota.

7. LACK OF RESPECT?

When the Vikings arrived in Houston for Super Bowl VIII, they immediately began to play the "nobody respects us" tune. Why? Well, while the Dolphins were assigned the Houston Oilers' practice facility, Minnesota's training site was a high school that was a twenty-minute bus ride from their hotel. The NFL said it was still a state-of-the-art facility, but the Vikings complained that the showers didn't work, there were sparrows' nests in the changing room, there were no lockers in the "locker" room, and the field had no tackling sleds. Bud Grant even complained to the commissioner's office that they were treating his team like they were in a "pickup game," a verbal swipe that earned the coach a fine from Pete Rozelle. Unfortunately, the Vikings couldn't find respect in Rice Stadium either, and the Dolphins thumped them, 24–7.

8. TURNOVERS

You can't win Super Bowls when you turn the ball over (see Buffalo, Super Bowl XXVII, and Oakland, Super Bowl XXXVII). The Vikings not only turned the ball over in their Super Bowl losses, they had crushing turnovers at key spots in pivotal portions of the games. In Super Bowl IV Charlie West fumbled a kick-off that gave the Chiefs possession on the 19-yard line. Six plays later the Chiefs were in the end zone, courtesy of Kansas City running back Mike Garrett, and had a commanding 16–0 lead. In Super Bowl VIII Minnesota turned it over only twice, but both came deep in Miami territory. First, Oscar Reed coughed up the ball on the 6-yard line, as the Vikings were trying to get on the board late in the second quarter. A touchdown there would have brought the Vikings within ten points. In the fourth quarter Tarkenton was intercepted at the goal line by Miami cornerback Curtis Johnson. Super Bowl IX brought more heartache for the Vikings. In the second quarter the Vikings were primed to take the lead over the Steelers. On a first-down play at the Pittsburgh 25-yard line, Tarkenton unloaded a pass inside the 5-yard line toward wide receiver John Gilliam, but Gilliam was met simultaneously by the ball and Steelers safety Glen Edwards. Edwards's hit knocked the ball up in the air for about as long as a punt, and it was picked off by Steelers defensive back Mel Blount. Later, running back Bill Brown fumbled the second-half kickoff, leading directly to a Pittsburgh touchdown and a 9–0 Steelers lead. Then early in the fourth quarter, running back Chuck Foreman fumbled at the Steelers' 7-yard line. Finally, in Super Bowl XI the big turnover occurred in the first quarter. After blocking a Ray Guy punt, Minnesota had a first-and-goal at the Oakland Raiders' 3-yard line. Then running back Brent McClanahan fumbled the ball away, and the Vikings' best chance to take a lead fizzled; they went on to lose, 32–14.

9. **PAUL KRAUSE**

The NFL's all-time interceptions leader, Paul Krause started at free safety for all four Vikings' Super Bowl losses. Appropriately, he had the only interception for Minnesota in those four games, when he picked off Chiefs tight end Lenny Dawson in Super Bowl IV. He also recorded a fumble recovery of Vikings running back Franco Harris in Super Bowl IX, and was particularly busy during Super Bowl VIII against Miami, with five first-half tackles as the Dolphins' running game penetrated deep into the Vikings' defense.

10. **ONE REAL OPPORTUNITY**

Despite being outgained on the ground, 245–17, the Vikings' one shot to win a Super Bowl came in Super Bowl IX. As mentioned above, the Minnesota team blew two scoring opportunities with turnovers deep in Pittsburgh territory and wasted another chance when Vikings kicker Fred Cox missed a 39-yard field goal. The Steelers helped as well, botching two first-half field goals that kept the game close. But when the Vikings got within 9–6 early in the fourth quarter, they allowed the Steelers to chew up six and a half minutes off the clock during a twelve-play drive, which culminated in a Terry Bradshaw touchdown pass to tight end Larry Brown.

The Bills Are Due

OK, so the Vikings proved that losing four Super Bowl games can be devastating, but how about losing four in a row? The Bills went zero for four from 1990 through 1993. Think about how difficult it is to just make it to four straight Super Bowls—only one other team, Miami, can claim to have gone to three in a row—but as great an accomplishment as getting there each time was, the Buffalo Bills always came home empty-handed.

1. **51–3**

The 1990 AFC Championship Game between the Buffalo Bills and the Los Angeles Raiders in Rich Stadium was over before fans could get warm in their seats. The Bills jumped all over the Raiders, scoring forty-one points in the first half alone. With the outcome all but decided, the second half was equal parts celebration and coronation. The Bills partied, the crowd celebrated, and when the final gun sounded, a confident group of Buffalo Bills had qualified for Super

Bowl XXV with a 51–3 win. The Bills had every reason to be confident: they seemed like an unstoppable locomotive. All that stood in their way to the world championship was the New York Giants.

2. BRUCE SMITH

During a loss to Miami early in the 1990 season, defensive lineman Bruce Smith was seen on the sideline vociferously complaining to head coach Marv Levy about Levy's decision to bench some of the Bills' starters. Later that year, before a regular season game with the Giants, he told reporters that it was time for Giants star Lawrence Taylor to step aside, so Smith could take the title of best defensive player in the game. Love him or hate him, Smith was one of the best at what he did, a proud warrior who valued winning above all else. His shining moment came in Super Bowl XXV, when he made a great individual effort to sack Giants quarterback Jeff Hostetler for a safety.

3. JIM KELLY

If a single player symbolized the Buffalo Bills from this era, it was their gunslinging quarterback from the University of Miami. Jim Kelly was a throwback, a player who wore his heart on his sleeve, never afraid to hide his emotion. He didn't have the strongest arm, but he always made the big throw; he wasn't the fleetest of foot but could scramble with the best of them when he needed a first down. Like the rest of his teammates, though, he never quite made the super play on Super Sunday. He was at his best driving the Bills at the end of Super Bowl XXV, getting them to the 30-yard line (not quite far enough). In Super Bowl XXVI he threw for 275 yards, but most of those were in garbage time, and he was picked off four times. He left Super Bowl XXVII with an injury, and in Super Bowl XXVIII he threw for 260 yards but only led a single touchdown drive.

4. **MARV LEVY**

Before he led the Bills to four Super Bowls, he was probably best known for an NFL Films sound bite in which he called an official an "over-officious jerk." Admit it, you've never heard anyone called over-officious, have you? A veteran coach and student of history, Marv Levy was just as comfortable telling reporters about historical battles as he was discussing game plans. Levy's previous Super Bowl experience was as an assistant under the Redskins' George Allen in Super Bowl VII. His coaching work earned him enshrinement in the Pro Football Hall of Fame.

5. **THE COMEBACK**

The Bills' string of four straight Super Bowl appearances would have been stopped at two were it not for a miraculous comeback in a playoff game against Houston in 1992. Houston safety Bubba McDowell returned an interception 58 yards early in the third quarter to give the Oilers a 35–3 lead in the AFC wild-card game. But the Bills, led by quarterback Frank Reich in place of an injured Jim Kelly, struck back quickly. A Kenneth Davis touchdown followed by a successful on-sides kick and a Reich touchdown pass to receiver Don Beebe made the score 35–17. Before the third quarter was done, Reich hooked up on two touchdowns with wide receiver Andre Reed to cut the score to 35–31. The Bills went on to win 41–38 in overtime. What people forget about the 1992 season is that the Bills still needed to win two more playoff games—at Pittsburgh and at Miami—to advance to the Super Bowl.

6. STEVE CHRISTIE

Steve Christie replaced Scott Norwood as Buffalo's placekicker in 1992. Christie had a strong leg, as evidenced by his Super Bowl–record 54-yard field goal in Super Bowl XXVIII. Although Norwood's miss in Super Bowl XXV still lingered, Christie kicked two big field goals in the playoff win over Houston listed above, including the overtime game-winner.

7. STEVE TASKER

Steve Tasker was the Bills' Pro Bowl special teams player. He and Giants defensive back Reyna Thompson were probably the two best kick and punt coverage men in the league. Tasker was there for every Super Bowl, even giving the Bills a glimmer of hope early in Super Bowl XXVII by blocking a Dallas punt that set up the first score of the game.

8. ANDRE REED

Andre Reed was the Bills' premier receiver and one of Jim Kelly's favorite targets. Following Super Bowl XXVIII, Reed was the all-time Super Bowl receptions leader with twenty-seven. The record was broken the following Super Bowl by Jerry Rice.

9. THE BILLS VS. THE NFC

From 1990 through 1993, when the Bills won four consecutive AFC championships, they played sixteen regular season games versus the NFC. Their record in those games was 14–2, including 4–1 in games against the three teams they faced in the Super Bowl. It should also be noted that the two losses were each in the final regular season contest, and both games were meaningless to the Bills, who had sewn up play-off berths. Yet, as we all know, their Super Bowl record against the NFC was 0–4.

10. **FOUR IN A ROW**

Four straight years in the Super Bowl is no mean feat. Look at baseball, for example: The Yankees went to four World Series in a row from 1998 to 2001, but the last time a baseball team made four consecutive Fall Classics was forty years ago—the Yankees again from 1960 to 1964. But baseball is different, as are hockey and basketball; for sure, it's harder in football. The last time an NFL team competed in four straight championship games was from 1951 through 1955 when the Browns played five in a row. But back then there were only twelve teams in the league, and two teams made the postseason; it was nothing like the marathon teams endure now.

Can You Believe It?

Many of the Super Bowl games have been sleep-inducing. Occasionally, though, a game will live up to the hype, and there is nothing better than a Super Bowl that comes down to the last few moments. Below are the ten most memorable Super Bowl finishes.

1. **SUPER BOWL XXXVI**

The New England Patriots were reeling, having squandered a 17–3 fourth-quarter lead to the St. Louis Rams. With the score tied, the Patriots marched 40 yards to set up a field goal attempt by Adam Vinatieri. Vinatieri had won their playoff game against Oakland with two big kicks in the snow, and now he had a championship riding on his leg. The 48-yard attempt was pure, and probably would have been good from 60 yards. He became the second kicker to win a Super Bowl at the last second and gave the Patriots their first world championship.

2. **SUPER BOWL XXXIV**

Just two seasons before, the Rams were involved in another nail-biter that came down to the last play—

Super Bowl XXXIV. They took a 23–16 lead over the Tennessee Titans with just under two minutes on the clock, then watched as quarterback Steve McNair led the Titans down the field on a remarkable two-minute drill. The Titans were at the 10-yard line with time left for just one more play; a touchdown would tie the game. McNair called a slant play for wide receiver Kevin Dyson, who caught the ball at the 5. It seemed to be a good call, since Dyson was isolated on linebacker Mike Jones, but Jones was up to the challenge. He wrapped Dyson around the waist and brought him down before the receiver could stretch the ball over the goal line. The Titans wound up 1 yard short, making the Rams the champs.

3. SUPER BOWL XXV

Buffalo's Scott Norwood had the opportunity to do something no other man has: kick a field goal on the game's final play to come up from behind for a Super Bowl win. (Vinatieri's kicks, it should be noted, came with the score tied.) The Bills trailed the Giants, 20–19, when they took possession at their own 8-yard line with two minutes remaining. Quarterback Jim Kelly and running back Thurman Thomas led a frantic drive that put the ball at the New York 30-yard line and brought on Norwood to attempt a game-winning 48-yard field goal. Norwood had not made a field goal of this distance on grass all season. (The Bills played their home games on artificial turf.) The kick was strong and had enough leg, but it wound up about 3 yards right of the goal posts, and the Giants ended up with the win.

4. SUPER BOWL XXIII

The 49ers and the Bengals went three quarters without an offensive touchdown between them, but some fourth-quarter fireworks turned Super Bowl XXIII into one of the most memorable of big game finishes. The 49ers were looking for their third championship in eight seasons, and trailing by three points late in the fourth quarter, they turned to their savior, quarterback Joe Montana. Montana led the best two-minute drill in Super Bowl history, starting at his own 8-yard line and culminating with his 10-yard touchdown pass to John Taylor with only thirty-nine seconds remaining. San Francisco sent Bill Walsh out as a winner in his final game as 49ers' head coach.

5. SUPER BOWL V

Super Bowl V was a dreadfully played game; there's no way around it. The Colts were trailing 13–6 in the fourth quarter when they took advantage of two Craig Morton interceptions. The first set up a Tom Nowatzke touchdown that tied the score for Baltimore. The second, by Colts linebacker Mike Curtis, came off a deflection and set up a 33-yard field-goal attempt by rookie kicker Jim O'Brien. O'Brien made the kick, and die-hard Colts fans everywhere rejoiced as their team redeemed themselves after their poor showing in Super Bowl III. His field goal also prompted Cowboys defensive lineman Bob Lilly to throw his helmet in frustration; flying about 40 yards, it was probably Dallas's best pass of the day.

6. SUPER BOWL VII

The final score, 14–7, was probably a little closer than the Miami Dolphins would have liked it, but their Super Bowl win was still the culmination of a perfect season. They did have to sweat at the end, though, as the Redskins scored a fluke touchdown off a blocked field goal when Miami's Garo Yepremian made an ill-advised attempt to pass the ball. The Redskins also got the ball back following a three-and-out, but they were out of timeouts and couldn't move the ball successfully. The Dolphins became the only team to go undefeated and untied and win the Super Bowl in the same season. It was a sweet ride off the field for head coach Don Shula.

7. SUPER BOWL II

Yes, Super Bowl II was a blowout, and no, there was nothing in the final minutes of game action that could be called "memorable." But after the final gun, things got special, as the victorious Green Bay Packers hoisted their stoic coach, Vince Lombardi, onto their shoulders for the final time. Even though rumors had been circulating that this could be Vince's final game, viewers didn't know for certain. The Green Bay players knew, however, and it made for an overwhelming emotional experience, one that you hope Packers fans enjoyed because they didn't win another Super Bowl for close to thirty years.

8. SUPER BOWL X

Earlier we discussed some questionable decision-making by Pittsburgh coach Chuck Noll in the later moments of Super Bowl X versus the Cowboys. Noll's decision not to attempt a punt with less than two minutes left put the Cowboys 61 yards from the Vince Lombardi Trophy. Two plays netted the Cowboys 23 yards and gave them an opportunity to take three cracks at the end zone. The first two passes fell incomplete, and with one last shot at glory, Dallas quarterback Roger Staubach heaved one into the end zone. Fans of both Pittsburgh and Dallas had to be reminded of three weeks earlier, when Staubach hooked up with wide receiver Drew Pearson on a Hail Mary play to knock Minnesota out of the playoffs. This time,

Pittsburgh defensive back Glen Edwards intercepted the pass and ran out the clock, preserving a 21–17 win and the Steelers' second consecutive championship.

9. SUPER BOWL XXXII

The conclusion of Super Bowl XXXII was one of the more memorable you'll see because the Green Bay defense allowed Denver to score a go-ahead touchdown with fewer than two minutes to play. With the score tied at twenty-four, the Broncos drove 50 yards to a first down on the Green Bay 1-yard line. Then, with no timeouts remaining, Green Bay had no way to stop the clock and no way to prevent the Broncos from running the clock down until a few seconds remained to kick the game-winning field goal. Instead, they allowed Broncos running back Terrell Davis to score untouched for a 31–24 lead. The Packers' Brett Favre led a furious rally, driving his team into Denver territory as the clock ticked down, but the magic ran out when his fourth-down pass for tight end Mark Chmura was broken up by linebacker John Mobley.

10. SUPER BOWL XXXVIII

A total of thirty-seven points, 427 yards of offense, a Super Bowl–record 85-yard touchdown pass, a touchdown with a little more than a minute left to tie the game, and a last-second field goal to win it—and that was just in the fourth quarter! Quarterback Jake Delhomme led the Carolina Panthers to come back from deficits of both fourteen and seven points, the New England Patriots drove the field for a late field-goal attempt, and Adam Vinatieri was the Patriots' hero once again, nailing a 41-yard field goal at the final gun to earn a 32–29 win.

Jon SooHoo

Brett Favre led a frantic final minute drive in Super Bowl XXXII, but his Green Bay Packers fell short, losing to Denver 31-24.

What's So Special?

Sometimes special teams seem like an afterthought (and anyone who watched the Giants under Jim Fassel understands this). But coaches always stress the three phases of the game: offense, defense, and special teams. In Super Bowl history special, and not so special, plays from the special teams have proven to be the difference.

1.   JON KASAY

The Carolina Panthers had just scored on a dramatic touchdown drive to tie the New England Patriots late in the fourth quarter of Super Bowl XXXVIII. With a little more than a minute to play, it looked for sure there would be an overtime Super Bowl for the first time. But then Carolina kicker Jon Kasay made the blunder of all special-teams blunders by shanking his kickoff out of bounds. By rule, the Patriots took over possession at their own 40-yard line. That gave Patriots quarterback Tom Brady all he needed to move his team into field-goal range, allowing Adam Vinatieri to win it for New England.

2. RON DIXON AND JERMAINE LEWIS

Super Bowl XXXV was a rather boring affair for two and a half quarters until Giants wide receiver Ron Dixon and the Ravens' Jermaine Lewis electrified the crowd with back-to-back kickoff return touchdowns. The Baltimore Ravens took a 17–0 lead over the New York Giants on cornerback Duane Starks's interception return for a touchdown, and just when the Giants looked like they were out of it, Dixon took the ensuing kickoff back 97 yards for a touchdown to cut their deficit to ten points. (Just a few weeks earlier, Dixon had scored on a kickoff against the Eagles in a playoff game.) As the momentum appeared to be leaning the Giants' way, Baltimore's Jermaine Lewis broke a few tackles and took New York's kickoff back 84 yards for the score that sealed the deal. The Ravens went on to win, 34–7.

3. DERRICK JENSEN

With Super Bowl XVIII scoreless in the first quarter, backup fullback Derrick Jensen made the play to give the Los Angeles Raiders a lead they never relinquished. He charged unimpeded on Washington Redskins punter Jeff Hayes, blocked the kick, and then chased the ball into the end zone, where he fell on it for the first points of the game. The momentum was fully with the Raiders, and they carried it on to a 38–9 victory.

4. BILL BROWN

The Minnesota Vikings trailed the Pittsburgh Steelers, 2–0, at the half of Super Bowl IX, and although

Minnesota's offense had not mustered much through the first thirty minutes, they were receiving the second-half kickoff. They received it alright, but reserve running back Bill Brown promptly coughed it up, and Steelers linebacker Marv Kellum recovered for Pittsburgh at the 30-yard line. Four plays later, Pittsburgh running back Franco Harris found the end zone, and the Steelers led, 9–0.

5. MATT BLAIR, TERRY BROWN, AND FRED COX

Oh, but the Vikings weren't done in Super Bowl IX after Bill Brown's fumble. Their special teams finally got them on the board early in the fourth quarter. With the Steelers facing a fourth down inside the Minnesota 10-yard line, linebacker Matt Blair blocked Bobby Walden's punt, and the ball rolled back into the end zone, where it took a fortuitous hop into the arms of safety Terry Brown. The extra point would have made it a two-point game, but Fred Cox botched the extra point, clanging it off the left upright. Those six were the only points the Vikings scored on that day.

6. REGGIE HARRISON

Early in the fourth quarter of Super Bowl X, the Pittsburgh Steelers trailed the Dallas Cowboys, 10–7, and they were floundering. But Reggie Harrison came out of obscurity to jolt the Steelers to life. The running back and special teams player blocked Dallas punter Mitch Hoopes's punt (the ball hit his facemask) through the end zone for a safety that cut the lead to 10–9. In their next three possessions, the Steelers scored twelve points on just fifteen plays. That was enough for Pittsburgh to hang on to win their second straight Super Bowl, 21–17.

7. JOHN FOX

With his Carolina Panthers trailing the New England Patriots in the fourth quarter of Super Bowl XXXVIII, head coach John Fox made a fateful decision. A 33-yard touchdown run by running back DeShaun Foster brought the Panthers within 21–16 with more than twelve minutes remaining. Fox opted to attempt the two-point conversion to get within three points of the lead. When the attempt was no good, the Panthers trailed by five, forcing Fox to go for two again just minutes later when wide receiver Muhsin Muhammad snuck behind the New England secondary for an 85-yard touchdown reception. The second conversion attempt also failed, so instead of being up three, the Pathers were only led by one. When New England scored a touchdown to put them ahead, 27–22, they went for two and converted. Had the score been 27–24, the Patriots would have kicked the extra point, and thus, New England's winning field-goal attempt would have tied the game, rather than won it.

8. FULTON WALKER

It took seventeen Super Bowls for a kickoff to be brought back for a touchdown, and Miami cornerback Fulton Walker had the honors. In fact, his second-quarter return of 98 yards gave the Dolphins a lead that they held on the Redskins until the fourth quarter. In this game Miami scored on Walker's kickoff return and a 76-yard reception by wide receiver Jimmy Cefalo. Those two touchdown plays accounted for more than half of Miami's total yardage for the game, which they lost, 27–17.

9. BRAD MAYNARD

When you're a punter and you're team is going up against the 2000 Baltimore Ravens' defense, you expect to have a busy day. And that's just what the New York Giants' Brad Maynard had in Super Bowl XXXV. Maynard set a Super Bowl record with eleven punts, breaking the record of Dallas's Ron Widby in Super Bowl V, who had punted nine times. Maynard's counterpart, Kyle Richardson, had ten punts in the game.

10. MARK SEAY

The San Diego Chargers had very little to celebrate in Super Bowl XXIX. They were given a total dressing-down by the 49ers, losing 49–26. But they did make history, though it's little consolation: wide receiver Mark Seay recorded the first successful two-point conversion in Super Bowl history, hauling in a pass from quarterback Stan Humphries in the fourth quarter. That tightened the score to 42–18.

Almost

Sometimes it's the smallest thing that separates one Super Bowl player from immortality—a stop at the 1-yard line, a fumble in a big spot, a drop. A lot of players have walked off the field wondering "what if I just . . ." Without picking on Jackie Smith or Scott Norwood, here are ten of the biggest almosts in Super Bowl history.

1. DUANE THOMAS

The Cowboys were all set to take full command of Super Bowl V. They held a seven-point third-quarter lead over the Colts and had the ball deep in Colts' territory after recovering a fumble on the second-half kickoff. A Dallas touchdown (and fourteen-point lead) would pretty much salt the game away, and after moving the ball to the 1-yard line, a touchdown seemed a mere formality. That's when fate and Duane Thomas met head-on. Thomas, the Cowboys' leading rusher, fumbled the ball on a hit by the Colts' Jerry Logan, and defensive back Jim Duncan recovered the ball for Baltimore. Instead of ensuring a commanding lead, the Cowboys did not score again, as the Colts came back for a 16–13 win.

2. ROD PERRY

Rod Perry and Pat Thomas combined with Nolan Cromwell to give the Rams one of the most imposing secondaries of the late 1970s, and the three were instrumental in the Rams coming within fifteen minutes of pulling off one of the biggest shockers in Super Bowl history. Los Angeles was clinging to a 19–17 lead over the heavily favored Pittsburgh Steelers in Super Bowl XIV. Early in the fourth quarter, Steelers quarterback Terry Bradshaw heaved a bomb in the direction of wide receiver John Stallworth, who was locked step for step with Perry in coverage. At the last moment, Perry lunged with one hand in an attempt to deflect the pass, but he missed the ball by inches, and Stallworth hauled it in for a 73-yard touchdown. A few minutes later Stallworth victimized Perry on a similar long pass to set up the touchdown that iced the Steelers' 31–19 win.

3. HERMAN EDWARDS

Super Bowl XV turned on a big play for the Oakland Raiders. In the second quarter the Raiders led the Philadelphia Eagles, 7–0. Oakland quarterback Jim Plunkett rolled to his left and appeared to have no receivers open, but he suddenly heaved a pass down the sideline in the area of two receivers, running back Kenny King and wide receiver Bob Chandler. Herman Edwards, the Philadelphia cornerback on that side of the field, was caught momentarily leaning the wrong way and barely missed getting a hand on Plunkett's pass. The ball fell into King's hands, and he had clear sailing down the sideline, with an escort from Chandler. His 80-yard touchdown gave Oakland a 14–0 lead en route to a 27–10 blowout.

4. PETE JOHNSON

In 1981 Johnson was the Bengals' chief offensive weapon. A bruising back, he was virtually unstoppable in short-yardage situations. In Super Bowl XVI the Bengals called on Johnson to slice into the San Francisco 49ers' third-quarter lead. Trailing 20–7, Cincinnati faced a fourth-and-one on the 5-yard line. Johnson took the ball and gained 2 yards to set up a first-and-goal. He got the call again and picked up another 2 yards to put the ball at the 1. A second-down rush was stopped for no gain. Following a third down pass for no gain, Johnson got the call again. All year, he'd come through, but this time, linebacker Jack Reynolds and the San Francisco defense stuffed him. Even more remarkably, the 49ers had only ten men on the field for the fourth-down play! The Johnson mystique was broken, the Cincinnati come-back attempt fizzled, and Johnson was never the same again.

5. KIM BOKAMPER

One of the leaders of Miami's "Killer Bees" in Super Bowl XVII, Kim Bokamper was involved in one of the great-est near misses in Super Bowl history. Despite being outplayed, the Dolphins were nursing a 17–13 lead over the Washington Redskins late in the third quarter. The Redskins had a first down on their own 18-yard line when quarterback Joe Theismann dropped back to pass. It appeared the Redskins were setting up a screen, but Bokamper disrupted the play with a heavy rush. Theismann tried to loft the ball over Bokamper's head, but Bokamper tipped the ball in the air with both hands. It looked as if the ball would fall right into the linebacker's hands, but Theismann alertly lunged forward and knocked the ball away to make an incompletion. This kept it to a four-point game, enabling the Redskins to stay close enough to salt the game away with two fourth-quarter touchdowns.

6. RICH KARLIS

In Super Bowl XXI the Broncos went into the half with a one-point lead over the New York Giants. But it could have been a lot more and Denver kicker Rich Karlis was one of the primary culprits. When a touchdown would have given them a ten-point lead early in the second quarter, the Broncos blew a first-and-goal opportunity on the 1-yard line. First, three plays lost them 3 yards, and Karlis trotted onto the field for a 23-yard chip shot, which he hooked badly left. Shortly thereafter, Denver was back deep in New York territory, and Karlis shanked another makable field goal, a 34-yarder. Anything under 40 yards should be automatic for an NFL kicker, and leaving those points on the board totally changed the complexion of the second half.

7. KEVIN DYSON

There can't be a bigger—or smaller—almost than coming up a yard short of the end zone on the game's final play when your team trails by seven points. Dyson was the Titans' receiver in Super Bowl XXXIV who was unable to shed a tackle by Rams linebacker

Mike Jones on the final play from scrimmage. Dyson ran his route precisely, but Jones made a great play to keep him out of the end zone.

8. LEWIS BILLUPS

Joe Montana has earned his reputation as one of the greatest and most clutch players in Super Bowl history: four starts, four wins, eleven touchdowns, and zero interceptions. Perhaps his signature moment came in Super Bowl XXIII, when he rallied the 49ers on a 92-yard drive with three minutes remaining to knock off the Cincinnati Bengals, 20–16. However, earlier in that fourth quarter, Bengals cornerback Lewis Billups had the opportunity to drive a stake into the heart of the Montana mystique. Trailing 13–6, Montana completed two passes for 71 yards to move the 49ers to the Cincinnati 14-yard line. On the next play Montana looked for John Taylor in the end zone, but the ball was a little underthrown. Billups stepped in front of Taylor for a sure interception, but the ball slipped through his hands, resulting in an incompletion. The next play, Montana hit Jerry Rice for the touchdown that tied the game.

9. THURMAN THOMAS

It was the Bills' final drive of Super Bowl XXV, and they faced a third-down-and-one at their own 19-yard line. Trailing the New York Giants by a point, the Bills hoped to move another 50 or so yards to get themselves in field goal range, and they almost got it back on one snap. The call was a draw play out of shotgun formation to Thomas, who ran up the middle and then left into the open field. Thomas was chewing up yardage, and the only thing that stood between him and a long, long gain was Giants cornerback Everson Walls. Walls, a ten-year veteran ball hawk who was not exactly remembered for his tackling, wrapped Thomas around the waist for a great solo tackle. Thomas gained 22 yards on the play, but without Walls it could have been a lot more. Consequently, Scott Norwood's game-winning field-goal attempt might have been shorter.

10. **RICKY PROEHL**

In the fourth quarter of Super Bowl XXXVI, the St. Louis Rams were looking for a hero. Outplayed through most of the game by the New England Patriots, they trailed by seven in the game's waning moments. Suddenly, their hero materialized in the form of wide receiver Ricky Proehl. With just under two minutes remaining, Kurt Warner hit Proehl on the left sideline near the 10-yard line. Proehl's stop and cut move enabled him to sneak inside the defense and into the end zone for a touchdown that covered 26 yards and tied the score. Unfortunately for the Rams, they left a little too much time on the clock for the Patriots, who marched down the field for Adam Vinatieri's game-winning field goal. Remarkably, just two seasons later, the same scene was replayed, this time with Proehl as a member of the Carolina Panthers. Proehl's 15-yard touchdown with 1:08 left drew Carolina even with New England. And just like in Super Bowl XXXVI, Vinatieri kicked a game-winner at the final gun.

And now
a Few Words . . .

The Super Bowl has become the most-watched television program every year not solely because of the action on the field. Many people tune in just to see the commercials. Each year the companies who can afford the exorbitant rates (a couple million dollars will get you a thirty second spot) premiere their new spots during the telecast. As you'll see from the two lists below, some commercials score a touchdown, but others have been disastrous fumbles. First, the best commercials.

1. APPLE COMPUTER

If the Rose Bowl is the granddaddy of all college bowl games, then the one-minute spot run by Apple for their new Macintosh during Super Bowl XVIII is the granddaddy of all Super Bowl commercials. The spot ran only once, but it accomplished more than Apple could have ever dreamed. The commercial's concept and impact make this the spot against which every other Super Bowl commercial is measured.

Dreary, dark, and directed by well-known filmmaker Ridley Scott, the Macintosh ad, which aired in January 1984, was a takeoff on George Orwell's *1984*, with a narrator droning on and on like Big Brother and the Automatons staring mouths agape until a blonde woman in a running outfit hurls a sledgehammer at Big Brother's screen, forcing it to explode. The triumph over Big Brother struck a chord in Americans, as Apple's sales goals were exceeded by more than 50 percent during the first three months after the commercial aired. Before this spot, the impact a commercial during the Super Bowl telecast could have was well known, but Apple ushered in the era of advertising-as-entertainment.

2.   COCA-COLA

Chances are, if you're over forty, you still remember Coke's historic commercials from the early 1970s. In one ad a crowd of young people, a cross section of the world's population, are gathered in a field, singing together, and of course, they're all drinking their favorite beverage—Coke. "I'd like to teach the world to sing, in perfect harmony." Few, however, remember that this spot first aired during Super Bowl VI in January 1972. The spot struck a nerve with a nation in the throes of the Vietnam War. The commercial, and the song, became international sensations. Come on, everybody now: "I'd like to buy the world a Coke, and keep it company."

3.   BUDWEISER

For about two months prior to Super Bowl XXIII in January 1989, Budweiser began running commercials

to hype their own Super Sunday campaign. But the
beer company had created more than a regular commercial; they planned to air a series of four commercials during the game—and they named them the Bud
Bowl. A simulated game pitting Budweiser longnecks
against Bud Light longnecks ended with Bud winning,
27–24, on a last-second field goal—a result that was
almost as anticipated as the final score of the 49ers-
Bengals Super Bowl. Bud became the most prominent
example of a company generating excitement for their
Super Bowl commercials before the game.

4. AMERICAN EXPRESS

"Do you know me?" That was the selling line of a
long-running American Express campaign in the
1970s. The commercials featured a celebrity (or at
least someone whose name was recognizable even if
his face wasn't) asking, "Do you know me?" and then
they continued on about the value of having the
American Express Card. The spokesman's card was
recognized everywhere, even if his face wasn't. The
first of these spots aired during Super Bowl VIII in
1974.

5. BUDWEISER

During Super Bowl XXIX in 1995, Budweiser made a
transition from its now-lagging Bud Bowl to a simple
spot that started a long-running campaign. It was pretty simple really: three frogs in a bog, with the lights
from a bar nearby. The frogs croaked out the name of
their brew of choice: "Bud," "Weis," "Er." The campaign aired for years with some new characters joining
in, including lizards Louie and Frankie, and a ferret.

6. MASTER LOCK

Master Lock aired only one television commercial every year, and it always came on during the Super Bowl. The tradition began in 1974, when Master spent $107,000 for their spot. It's an ad I'm sure you remember. A Master Lock is held up in a bull's-eye, and a bullet pierces the lock. Even though a hole forms in the lock, it doesn't come unlocked. The concept was simple, but the message was clear: A Master Lock can withstand anything. The company continued with its one spot per year plan until 1996.

7. MONSTER.COM

One of the few companies to survive the dot-com boom and bust, job search engine Monster.com used kids in one of the funnier Super Bowl spots in the last decade. For the 1999 Super Bowl, their campaign was called "When I Grow up," and it featured children telling what they wanted for their future. No one said, "I want to be a doctor" or "I want to be a lawyer." Instead, they made statements like "I want to have a brown nose" and "I want to claw my way to middle management" and "I want to be a yes man." When the commercial finished, viewers were directed to Monster's site, where the options are a little better.

8. M&M's

There's an old urban legend that green M&M's serve as aphrodisiacs. In Super Bowl XXXI the M&M's spots had a little fun with this myth. In one spot Dennis Miller asks the green M&M's character if everything they say about the green M&M's is true. In another she walks down the street as bystanders hoot and whistle at her. And in a third someone walks in on her in her dressing room with her shell off, and she quickly tries to cover herself up.

9. FEDERAL EXPRESS

What happens when you don't use Federal Express and instead opt for a cut-rate delivery service? This choice was the theme of FedEx's 1999 spots, which featured the Detroit Red Wings, who had just won the Stanley Cup, and their crowd of fans eagerly awaiting the cup presentation. But when they open up the package meant to contain the cup, they find a bag of burro food. There's that cut-rate service for you. Where was the real Stanley Cup? In Bolivia, of course, at the residence of one Jose Luis Arena, who had the cup featured at his market stand as "El Especial de Hoy." The message is clear: When you need to get something delivered, go with Federal Express.

10. E*TRADE FINANCIAL

By Super Bowl XXXV in 2001, it was obvious that the dot-com boom of the late 1990s was over. In the previous years a number of on-line start-ups—with little capital to speak of—seemed to throw their money at Super Bowl spots, and several of those companies paid dearly for it in the long run. E*Trade's message in Super Bowl XXXV was simple: Invest wisely. They chose to get the message across by having their mascot (a monkey) moseying on a horse through a ghost town—a ghost town filled with the dot-com businesses that had recently gone under.

Where's the Beef?

So who had the biggest fumbles in Super Bowl history? No, not Duane Thomas and Jim Kelly. We're talking about the companies who shelled out big bucks to run their commercial on the biggest stage, only to have it panned like a disastrous Broadway opening night.

1. REEBOK

Okay, so the "Dan and Dave . . . See You in Barcelona" commercials that Reebok ran during Super Bowl XXVI in January 1992 weren't truly terrible. They were just not very prophetic. Dan O'Brien and Dave Johnson were the premier American hopefuls for the decathlon at the 1992 Barcelona Summer Olympics. O'Brien, in fact, was regarded as one of the best decathletes in the world and was a favorite to win the gold. So Reebok had the idea to launch a campaign during the Super Bowl that they hoped would carry them through the Olympics. The ads focused on the two as youngsters and followed them in their careers, asking "Who is the world's greatest athlete? Find out in Barcelona." One minor problem: the American decathlon trials had yet to be held. Sure enough, O'Brien choked at the trials and didn't even make the team, and Johnson qualified for the Olympics but some wondered if he would even medal. O'Brien stayed home, and Johnson won the bronze. So who was the world's greatest athlete? Robert Zmelik of Czechoslovakia. No word on whether he wore Reeboks.

2. JUST FOR FEET

Just for Feet ran an ad in Super Bowl XXXIII that was almost universally panned for its poor taste. Here's the story: A handful of military-looking men in a truck track a barefoot Kenyan running through the country- side. (We know he's Kenyan by the jacket he wears.) The military men give him drugged water, and when he subsequently passes out, they force sneakers onto his feet. The Kenyan wakes up confused and tries to kick the shoes off. The tag line? "To preserve and pro- tect feet." Just for Feet should have worried about preserving their reputation. They sued FOX, the net- work that broadcast the game, for moving the spot to the fourth quarter, and then their ad agency, Saatchi and Saatchi, for selling them on the ad in the first place. Saatchi responded with a lawsuit of its own. Just a few years later, Just for Feet filed for Chapter 11.

3. CRYSTAL PEPSI

Pepsi has had some great spots over the years, but their Super Bowl XXVII ad, which launched their new Crystal Pepsi, was a bore. This spot used Van Halen's *Right Now* as its theme. If they were going to use a

Van Halen song, couldn't they have used one from their glory years with David Lee Roth instead of the 1990s Sammy Hagar Van Halen? Crystal Pepsi turned out to be as forgettable as this commercial, as people stayed away from the clear cola in droves.

4. THE DOT-COM BOWL

Super Bowl XXXIV in January 2000 was known as the Dot-Com Bowl; nearly 50 percent of the advertisers were something dot-com. Not long after January 2000, many of those dot-coms had been flushed. Yes, there are mainstays, including Monster and HotJobs, but back then there were other new Web sites that felt like they had to make a monumental impact—whether they could handle the financial hit or not. Remember OurBeginning.com? Computer.com? Netpliance? LifeMinders? Epidemic.com? Didn't think so.

5. APPLE

The folks at Apple tried to catch lightning in a bottle two years in a row. Following their monumental "Big Brother" spot from Super Bowl XVIII, they were back for the next game with a commercial titled "Lemmings." Trying to build interest in their new business system, Apple once again went with dark imagery, as a line of suited businessman wearing blindfolds whistle along in conformity until one renegade removes his blindfold to look for a different path. Consumers didn't connect with this spot, though, and Apple wasn't ready to supply what was promised. Thousands of employees were eventually laid off, and company founder Steve Jobs was soon shown the door. It was more than a decade later before Apple advertised during the Super Bowl again.

6. ENERGIZER

Energizer has had a nice run with its pink bunny, who's "still going." But before the folks at Energizer brought the bunny to television, they employed the annoying Australian Jacko as their spokesman in a spot during Super Bowl XXII. Remember this guy? He looked a little like a football player, had spiked blond hair, and appeared to have an aversion to toothbrushes. He also yelled a lot and destroyed things. Supposedly, he was a celebrity in Australia, although I can't imagine why. Then again, so were Paul Hogan and Yahoo Serious. Go figure.

7. BUDWEISER

Many people liked it, but Super Bowl XXXIV's Budweiser "Whassup!" ads could really grate on you quickly. A bunch of friends greeted each other with "whassup!" constantly—that's the commercial, folks. The message, I guess, was that Bud brings camaraderie. That's fine, but following this commercial, society had to endure average folks on the street saying "whassup" whenever they were greeted by a simple "hello." I'm still trying to get over that.

8. CADILLAC

Can you ever go wrong with a commercial starring Cindy Crawford in her prime? Cadillac found a way in their Super Bowl XXXI spot for the Catera. The convoluted story is this: Cindy is a princess stuck in a castle, and as we all know, all princesses look like supermodels and dress in skimpy black leather outfits. In order to get more fun in her life, a wizard in the form of a red duck (you read that right) gives her the keys to the Catera. Critics howled that this was sexist and beneath Cadillac. Apparently someone else agreed, as the commercial was ditched shortly after it first aired on Super Sunday.

9. NIKE

Dennis Hopper sneaks into a locker room and starts smelling Buffalo Bills defensive end Bruce Smith's Nikes. What will happen if Smith discovers Hopper? In Hopper's words, "Bad things, man. Bad things." My sentiments exactly.

10. SUBWAY

Am I the only one sick of this Jared guy? You know him, he weighed about four hundred pounds before he discovered that eating Subway sandwiches for lunch and dinner every day, combined with a healthy dose of walking, helped him lose weight. This was years ago, and I applaud the guy for keeping the weight off. But he continues to be a Subway spokesman. In Super Bowl XXXVII Subway brought Jared back to hawk their new sandwich. The ad features Jared imagining a Subway right in his living room. The irony is striking: Jared, who lost all his weight by walking to and from Subway, imagines having a Subway down the hall. No word on whether he also imagines himself a couple of hundred pounds heavier.

Stay Tuned

Once the Super Bowl became a television ratings winner, the networks realized that post–Super Bowl was a plum time slot. Some networks went with debut shows, while others went with more established shows to reinvigorate audiences. And just as in advertising, there were some successes and some colossal bombs. Take a trip down memory lane with ten shows that hit the airwaves after the Super Bowl signed off: five memorable and five forgettable.

1. *THE A-TEAM*

"If you have a problem, if no one else can help, and if you can find them, maybe you can hire the A-Team." A guilty pleasure that premiered as a two-hour pilot on NBC following Super Bowl XVII, *The A-Team* followed a squad of four Vietnam veterans who were wanted by the government for crimes they did not commit while they served overseas. They acted as mercenaries to help little guys everywhere right the wrongs of the

world. A great ensemble cast led by George Peppard as Col. Hannibal Smith and Mr. T as B. A. Barracus, drove this series through five successful seasons.

2. *SURVIVOR: THE AUSTRALIAN OUTBACK*

Survivor became a runaway hit for CBS in the summer of 2000. One of the earliest reality television shows, Survivor placed sixteen average Americans in a remote location, and with each episode, one survivor was voted off the island. In the end a jury of seven castaways voted on a sole survivor. CBS immediately signed on for another season following the show's initial success, and season two premiered after Super Bowl XXXV. More than forty-five million people stuck around following the game to watch episode one, as prison guard Debb from the Kucha tribe was the first castaway sent packing. How important was the Super Bowl in this show's ratings? After the forty-five million tuned in for the post-game episode, episode two's audience dropped by more than fifteen million viewers.

3. *THE WONDER YEARS*

A show that at first glance was hard to define made its debut on ABC following Super Bowl XXII in January 1988. Was *The Wonder Years* a comedy, a drama, or a family program? It turned out that the adventures of young Kevin Arnold and his family and friends spanned each of those genres and more. The story struck a chord with Boomers, the Vietnam generation, and young people everywhere. *The Wonder Years* lasted six seasons but couldn't survive Kevin's getting older. The show just wasn't cute anymore when Kevin looked like he was more than six feet tall and no longer fit into his throwback Jets jacket.

4. *HOMICIDE: LIFE On THE STREET*

NBC premiered this show following Super Bowl XXVII in January 1993 to critical acclaim. That was one of *Homicide*'s problems: Critics loved the show, but it only found a small core audience of fans who loved it intensely enough to keep the show on the air until 1999. But it was never a huge ratings-grabber for NBC. An inside look at the homicide division in Baltimore, it offered a phenomenal cast: Andre Braugher, Yaphet Kotto, Richard Belzer, Ned Beatty, Isabella Hoffman, Giancarlo Esposito.

5. *60 MINUTES*

CBS had a blowout with Super Bowl XXVI, as the Redskins routed the Buffalo Bills, 37–24, but they scored big with an abbreviated edition of their long-time ratings winner *60 Minutes*, when Steve Kroft sat down with presidential candidate Bill Clinton and his wife Hillary. Clinton was hardly the Democratic front-runner at the time; his campaign was starting to come apart at the seams, as allegations of sexual misconduct in Mr. Clinton's past surfaced. The Clintons' appearance on *60 Minutes* began a change in the momentum of the campaign, with Hillary Clinton vehemently protesting the allegations against her husband and even angering country music fans by saying she wouldn't "stand by her man" like Tammy Wynette. The rest is history.

6. *MACGRUDER AND LOUD*

ABC decided to follow their first-ever Super Bowl by airing the pilot of this police drama. In the series two partners, one man and one woman, become lovers and marry. As nice as their relationship is, department regulations dictate that partners can't be married, so they decide to keep their nuptuals their little secret. Starring John Getz and Kathryn Harrold (who?), this show was a secret to most Americans, who stayed away from it in big numbers. *MacGruder and Loud* lasted only fifteen episodes and three months.

7. *BROTHERS AND SISTERS*

In January 1979 NBC launched this forgettable comedy to try and capture some of the magic of the previous year's big screen *Animal House*. (CBS tried the same thing with *Delta House*, which also bombed.) *Brothers and Sisters*, starring Larry Anderson and Randy Brooks (don't ask me), lasted only twelve episodes before getting the hook.

8. *THE LAST PRECINCT*

Seven years after failing to capture the audience of a wildly popular movie with *Brothers and Sisters*, NBC still hadn't learned its lesson, debuting *The Last Precinct* following Super Bowl XX. This comedy, starring Adam West of *Batman* fame (this in and of itself should tell you something), tried to take advantage of the success of the *Police Academy* movies, with dismal results. The show lasted only a month. Here's a question to ponder, which stunk up the NBC airwaves more: this show or the Patriots in their 46–10 loss to the Bears?

9. *GRAND SLAM*

CBS must have figured that a baseball show would be perfect, considering the recent success Hollywood had

had with the films *Bull Durham*, *Major League*, and *Eight Men Out*. They followed Super Bowl XXIV with the worst television show about baseball since CBS's forgettable *Ball Four* in the seventies. This one was a little more fortunate than *The Last Precinct*. It lasted two whole months.

10. *HARD COPY*

This is not the *Hard Copy* newsmagazine program that premiered in 1989, but a drama about life in a newsroom that debuted on CBS following Super Bowl XXI. CBS execs must have thought that a program, starring Wendy Crewson, Dean Devlin, and Fionulla Flanagan (yes, those are real names), could carry a prime time slot. Well, no one else thought it could, and CBS said goodbye to *Hard Copy* at the end of its first season.

They Brought Us the Game

The list of men who have broadcast the Super Bowl is a who's who of broadcasting and former NFL legends. And considering how so many Super Bowls have been uncompetitive, the men below have needed to use all of their verbal skills to keep the masses entertained.

1. PAT SUMMERALL

Former Giants placekicker Pat Summerall is the dean of Super Bowl broadcasters, having called seventeen games. Working for both CBS and, then later, FOX, Summerall has acted both in analyst and play-by-play roles. He began broadcasting the NFL with CBS in 1962 and called his first Super Bowl in Super Bowl II, working alongside Ray Scott and Jack Kemp. Always subdued and never over-dramatic, Summerall is best remembered for his two-decade partnership with analyst John Madden. The duo called eight Super Bowls together, including the Patriots' unforgettable win over the Rams in Super Bowl XXXVI.

2. CURT GOWDY

The legendary host of *The American Sportsman* could also be known as the American Sportscaster. Through the course of his long career, he broadcast fifteen seasons of Boston Red Sox baseball, and covered seven Olympic Games, sixteen World Series, and eight Super Bowls as NBC's lead play-by-play man. He's also got a Peabody Award to his credit and resides in the broadcaster's wing of the Baseball Hall of Fame. Gowdy was on hand to call three landmark games: Super Bowl I, the Jets' upset in Super Bowl III, and the culmination of the Dolphins' perfect season in Super Bowl VII.

3. DICK ENBERG

Tennis, college basketball, college football, golf, the Olympic Games, boxing, horse racing, and, of course, the NFL. This just scratches the surface of the wonderful career of Dick Enberg, a man who's won thirteen Emmy Awards and has been inducted into the National Broadcasters Hall of Fame. And who could forget his roles in *Gus the Mule* and *The Naked Gun*? Enberg was a versatile play-by-play man for eight NBC Super Bowls, working with analysts from Merlin Olsen to Paul Maguire and Phil Simms. Enberg was also at the mike when John Elway finally snapped his Super Bowl hex in Super Bowl XXXII.

4. JOHN MADDEN

When it comes to NFL game analysts, Madden is in a league by himself. Since 1980 Madden's love for the game has shown through with every play, replay, and telestrator drawing. As the only Super Bowl–winning coach (he led the Raiders in Super Bowl XI) later to broadcast a Super Bowl game, Madden offers a fresh insight into the mind of coaches. A thirteen-time Emmy winner, Madden has been at the mike for nine Super Bowls on three networks. He's worked eight Super Bowls with long-time partner Pat Summerall, including Joe Montana's first (Super Bowl XVI) and the Patriots' stunning win over the Rams in Super Bowl XXXVI. In broadcasting Super Bowl XXXVII on ABC, Madden became the only man to call consecutive games on different networks. Madden has taken his celebrity seriously—he's the author of four *New York Times* bestselling books, and his annual NFL video game is widely considered the best by fans.

5. RAY SCOTT

A long-time radio voice for the Green Bay Packers, Scott was hired by CBS to be its number one NFL voice, paired with Pat Summerall. Scott was there at the Los Angeles Coliseum for Super Bowl I, one of the four games he called. He called three of his Super Bowls with Summerall.

6. AL MICHAELS

It's virtually impossible to think of ABC Sports without thinking of the multiple-Emmy-winning Al Michaels. His tenure at the network dates back to 1976, when as a thirty-one year old, he was brought on to anchor the network's baseball broadcasts. Ten years later he moved into the booth for *Monday Night Football*, where he has resided ever since. In addition, he's called or anchored coverage of golf, the NHL playoffs, the Indianapolis 500, and of course, the event for which he's become most famous, the USA hockey team's gold medal finish in the 1980 Winter Olympics. Michaels has called five Super Bowls for ABC, including two with perhaps the best finishes: the Giants' 20–19 win over the Bills in Super Bowl XXV and the Rams' 23–16 win over the Titans in Super Bowl XXXIV.

7. FRANK GIFFORD

Mr. Monday Night Football, Frank Gifford actually called his first Super Bowl with Ray Scott for CBS in Super Bowl I. He went on to call four more Super Bowls with ABC, including the network's first, Super Bowl XIX, for which he was the play-by-play voice.

8. MERLIN OLSEN

A member of the Los Angeles Rams' Fearsome Foursome defensive front in the late 1960s and early 1970s, Olsen went on to dual careers with NBC in the late '70s: as an actor on *Little House on the Prairie* and as the network's lead NFL analyst. Teamed primarily with play-by-play man Dick Enberg, Olsen called five Super Bowls, including Joe Montana's thrilling drive to win Super Bowl XXIII.

9. PHIL SIMMS

With Super Bowl XXXVIII in 2004, Simms called his fourth big game in eight years, two for NBC and two for CBS. Simms is now the leader of the pack for former Super Bowl quarterbacks who are now broadcasters. Five men have started Super Bowls at quarterback and later moved up to the booth to call the game. Simms, with his four games, has more under his belt than Boomer Esiason, Joe Theismann, Bart Starr, and Bob Griese, who've broadcast one each.

10. **TOM BROOKSHIER**

Trivia question: Who was Pat Summerall's analyst before John Madden? Answer: Tom Brookshier. Brookshier was a great defensive back for the Eagles back in the 1950s and 1960s; in fact, his number 40 was retired by the team. Following retirement, Brookshier went into television, doing work with CBS and NFL Films. Working alongside Summerall, Brookshier called three Super Bowls, including Super Bowl X.

We Didn't Come Here Looking for Trouble . . .

The 1985 Chicago Bears were like a traveling sideshow. There were new stories coming out of Chicago every week: the fat rookie, the winning streak, the defense, the music video. You name it; they took part in it. But they also won, and they did so emphatically. There's probably a great book to be written about this team, but for the time being, here's a top ten list.

1. "THE SUPER BOWL SHUFFLE"

If you can get your hands on this video, do so. Two months before the Super Bowl, the Bears recorded a song (and produced a video) for charity titled "The Super Bowl Shuffle." The fact that they put this together before they had even started the playoffs tells you all you need to know about the confidence of this team. Walter Payton, Jim McMahon, Steve Fuller, Willie Gault, Richard Dent, Refrigerator Perry, Mike Singletary, Otis Wilson, Gary Fencik, and Mike

Richardson all had singing parts (if you want to call them that). *"Well, they call me Sweetness, and I like to dance. . . . Running the ball is like making romance. . . . We had the goal since training camp, to bring Chicago a Super Bowl champ."* Priceless.

2. THE QUEST FOR PERFECTION

After an unexpected struggle with Tampa Bay in week one at Soldier Field and a dramatic comeback win in week three at Minnesota, where Jim McMahon came off the bench to throw three long touchdown passes, the Bears stomped over nine more opponents before a Monday night game in Miami against the Dolphins. The Bears had won their previous three games by a combined score of 104–3, but the Dolphins, with history—and members of their perfect 1972 Super Bowl champions—on their side, took down the Bears, 38–24, on *Monday Night Football*. McMahon missed the game, but that was the last time anyone even came close to the Bears for the rest of the season.

3. THE DEFENSE

Led by defensive coordinator Buddy Ryan, the Bears and their aggressive 46 defense dominated teams all season. Counting the playoffs and the Super Bowl, the Bears played nineteen games. They allowed more than ten points in just five of them. Mike Singletary, Otis Wilson, Richard Dent, Dan Hampton, and Dave Duerson went to the Pro Bowl, and Gary Fencik and Wilbur Marshall merited serious consideration. How good was the defense on the whole? They led the league in points allowed, rushing defense, overall defense, interceptions, and takeaways/giveaways.

4. MIKE DITKA AND BUDDY RYAN

With number four on the list, we're finally getting around to the head coach. Mike Ditka was a Bears' hero. A Hall of Fame tight end with Chicago and Dallas, Ditka came home to the Bears in 1982 and quickly turned things around. By year three, the team made the NFC Championship Game, and by year four, 1985, he had the best team in football. But not all the accolades went to Ditka. Buddy Ryan led the Bears' dominant defense, though neither coach could stand the other. Ryan and Ditka were known to battle it out, both in meetings and in the media. Ryan wanted all the credit for the defense; he felt Ditka was more of a hindrance than anything. Ditka, a notorious hothead, felt Ryan got too much of the credit for the team's success. It should be noted that both men were carried off the field following their Super Bowl victory. Ryan left the team in 1986 to become head coach of the Eagles, but he never made the Super Bowl as a head coach; in fact, his Eagles teams never won a single playoff game.

5. THE HEADBANDS

Who would have thought headbands could cause so many headaches? It started with the divisional playoff game against the New York Giants. Bears quarterback Jim McMahon wore a headband that bore the name of his sneaker company of choice. NFL commissioner Pete Rozelle was not amused and fined McMahon. McMahon, who was never known to back down from a challenge, came back the following week in the NFC championship with "ROZELLE" scribbled on his headband, causing another stir. Once the Super Bowl came around, McMahon was wearing headbands that drew attention to children's charities and an ailing friend.

6. THE MOONING

With the Ditka/Ryan conflict in full view, the Bears weren't exactly known for team harmony. Jim McMahon caused a bit of controversy during Super Bowl week, when he complained that the Bears wouldn't fly his acupuncturist to New Orleans to help the quarterback with his sore rear end. Before the Bears relented, McMahon dropped his pants and mooned a news helicopter, to show them, as he later described, where it hurt. The acupuncturist flew down, and McMahon miraculously felt better. He scored two touchdowns in the game.

7. THE SWAGGER

Not only were the Bears good, they knew they were good. And they weren't afraid to tell anyone about it. There was the "Shuffle," as we mentioned earlier, but there was so much more. Defensive lineman Dan Hampton: "[New England quarterback Tony Eason] was scared to death, and all we had to do was get to him early and the game would be over." Defensive back Dave Duerson: "We're the best of all time."

8. THE FRIDGE

William Perry was a rookie defensive tackle out of Clemson who, let's not mince words, had a little extra girth than may have been necessary. But he had an infectious smile, took up a lot of space in the middle of the line, and made for a great story. His legend grew during a Monday night game versus Green Bay in week seven at Soldier Field. With the offense knocking on the door of the end zone, Perry lined up as a full-back, took a handoff, and plunged in for a touchdown. A few weeks later in Green Bay, he caught a touch-down pass out of a similar formation. The Fridge capped his storybook season with a touchdown run in Super Bowl XX.

9. WALTER PAYTON

He was the greatest Bear, and he was always classy, so football fans everywhere had to smile that Walter Payton finally won his Super Bowl. After being so good for so long, on so many bad Bears teams, the man they called Sweetness reached the height of the sport. Many fans and media members complained loudly that Payton did not get a touchdown in the Super Bowl against the Patriots, while William Perry did. But those complaints never came from Payton, who retired in 1987 as the NFL's all-time leading rusher.

10. 46–10

It was an incredible performance to cap an incredible season. Following a fumble on the second play from scrimmage in Super Bowl XX, the Bears spotted the Patriots a field goal in the first quarter. Chicago then proceeded to score the next forty-four points, chasing one quarterback and holding New England to just 7 yards rushing. Their defense recorded six takeaways and seven sacks and scored on an interception return and a safety.

The Super Bowl's Real Most Wanted

Chances are you saw the title of this book and thought it referred to FOX's *America's Most Wanted*. Well, thankfully, we can't fill up a whole book on Super Bowl stars who've done time in the clink. But even Super Bowl athletes have had their share of legal trouble.

1. RAY LEWIS

Baltimore linebacker Ray Lewis was a spectator at Super Bowl XXXIV in Atlanta, one of many current NFL players in town to enjoy the experience, the game, and especially the parties. When the game was over, Lewis and a number of friends hopped in a limousine headed for one of the more exclusive nightclubs in the city. What happened after Lewis left the club is subject to some debate. Two men were stabbed to death in a brawl, and Lewis contended that even though he was there he had no direct involvement in the altercation. However, the linebacker and his friends did speed away from the scene in his limo. Lewis and two other men were brought up on murder charges, but the evidence against the football star was flimsy. He pled guilty to charges of obstruction in exchange for testimony against his co-defendants. Lewis came back to the Super Bowl one year later, humbled by the experience, and won the Super Bowl MVP award.

2. STANLEY WILSON

Running back Stanley Wilson helped the Cincinnati Bengals advance to Super Bowl XXIII by rushing for 74 yards and two touchdowns in their playoff wins over Seattle and Buffalo, and Wilson figured to be an important back for the Bengals when they went up against the San Francisco 49ers in the big game. But the night before the Super Bowl, he went on a cocaine binge. Police discovered Wilson in a drug-induced haze, but somehow he slipped away from an arrest and could not be found. Many of the Bengals were informed of the events of the preceding night, but most took the field not knowing what had become of their teammate. Wilson never played another down in the NFL. In fact, some of his teammates never saw him face-to-face after that night.

3. LEN DAWSON

Chiefs quarterback Len Dawson was not a criminal, but when you're under investigation by the FBI in the days leading up to the big game, there has to be a story. On the Tuesday before the Super Bowl, an NBC report quickly gained steam that Lenny Dawson had been linked to a well-known Detroit gambler named Donald "Dice" Dawson, who was no relation. Although the story made national news, it was really much ado about nothing, as other than a casual conversation on one or two occasions, the two Dawsons did not associate. And there was no hint of evidence that Lenny Dawson had ever even gambled. The distractions sure didn't bother him, though, as he led his Chiefs to a Super Bowl win over the Vikings with an MVP performance.

4. EUGENE ROBINSON

Eugene Robinson's story was more sad than anything else. The Atlanta Falcons had come out of nowhere to go 14–2 in the 1998 season, and then they upset the heavily favored Minnesota Vikings in the NFC Championship Game. This was due, in some part, to the leadership brought by the veteran safety Robinson, who was in his first year with the team following a number of successful seasons with the Packers. Robinson was one of the NFL's good guys, earning awards for all his off-field work with charities. His altruism made it all the more confusing that he skipped curfew the night before Super Bowl XXXIII and was arrested for soliciting a prostitute, who happened to be an undercover officer. Robinson was released from custody quickly and played in the game, but Falcons fans probably wish he hadn't; he was burned on the game-turning 80-yard touchdown pass from Broncos quarterback John Elway to receiver Rod Smith.

5. DON SHULA

No, Don Shula was not involved in any criminal activity, but he was part of one of the stranger crimes in Super Bowl history. Following his Dolphins' historic win in Super Bowl VII to cap an undefeated season, Shula was given the traditional ride on his players' shoulders. Storybook ending, right? Not necessarily. A thief stole Shula's watch right from his wrist. The coach got down off his players, chased the guy down, and got the timepiece back, making the thief just one more opponent who Shula got the best of.

6. MERCURY MORRIS

Don Shula did not get himself in trouble with the law, but one of the members of his perfect 1972 team did—and running back Mercury Morris paid dearly for it. Following his retirement, Morris slid into drug addiction, culminating in a guilty plea to selling cocaine to an undercover cop. Morris spent three years in jail and later became a sought-after speaker on the dangers of drugs.

7. MARK CHMURA

Say you're a thirty-year-old man with a wife and children at home. And let's also speculate that you're a universally respected professional athlete. Would you spend an evening at a post-prom party with a bunch of teenagers? Probably not. But that's what Mark Chmura did, hanging out and drinking at a neighbor's house on the night of said neighbor's high school prom. A seventeen-year-old girl charged Chmura, the Packers' tight end in Super Bowls XXXI and XXXII, with sexual assault and child enticement. Chmura was acquitted, but his career was ruined, and he retired shortly thereafter.

8. RAFAEL SEPTIEN

Rafael Septien was the Cowboys' placekicker for nearly a decade, including their Super Bowl XIII loss to the Pittsburgh Steelers. In fact, it was his field goal that cut Pittsburgh's lead to 21–17 immediately following

Cowboys tight end Jackie Smith's dropped pass. Following the 1986 season, Septien made headlines in a much more disturbing way: He was arrested for sexually assaulting a ten-year-old girl. He pled to a lesser charge and received ten years probation, and then had the audacity to complain about his treatment by the Cowboys when they cut him from their roster.

9. NATE NEWTON

A starting guard for the Cowboys' championship teams of the nineties, Nate Newton was pulled over twice in little over a month. What's so strange about that, you ask? In each instance, police found a little something extra in Nate's car. The first time they turned up more than 200 pounds (pounds!) of marijuana. The next bust turned up only a little more than 170 pounds of weed. Facing upwards of twenty years in prison, Newton pled to a lesser charge and was sentenced to thirty months.

10. MICHAEL IRVIN

Why not another Cowboy to round out the list? The Cowboys' number-one receiver on their three championship teams in Super Bowls XXVII, XXVIII, and XXX, Michael Irvin was busted for a little partying in a Dallas hotel room in 1996. The police found Irvin with marijuana, cocaine, and two topless dancers, neither of whom (shock!) was his wife. The Dallas receiver went on trial but pled no contest to the cocaine possession charge. He was sentenced to four years probation, a five-game suspension from the NFL, a severe case of egg on his face, and oh yeah, had a contract put out on his life. In a weird sidebar to the case, a Dallas cop was arrested for trying to hire a hit man to have Irvin killed. Apparently, this cop's girlfriend was one of Irvin's companions in the hotel room.

Put Me Back In

Injuries are a part of football, but no team likes to be shorthanded in the big game. Super Bowl teams have been dealing with injured players since the first series of Super Bowl I. Here are some of the more memorable injuries in Super Bowl history.

1. TIM KRUMRIE

The most memorable single injury to occur during a Super Bowl game happened just minutes after San Francisco offensive lineman Steve Wallace left Super Bowl XXIII with a broken leg. The Bengals' Tim Krumrie, one of Cinncinati's best defenders, broke his leg in two places. Thanks to NBC's numerous replays, the images of this injury are hard to forget. Krumrie was taken to the locker room but insisted on staying to watch the game before doctors transported him to a local hospital.

2. PHIL SIMMS

New York quarterback Phil Simms was injured late in the 1990 season in a game at Giants Stadium against the Buffalo Bills. Simms was lost for the remainder of the season, and it appeared the Giants' Super Bowl chances had been lost as well. But the New York team rode backup quarterback Jeff Hostetler to an upset win over the 49ers in the NFC Championship Game and then faced those same Bills in Super Bowl XXV. Hostetler played a magical game as the Giants won their second world championship in five years.

3. BOYD DOWLER

On the third play of Super Bowl I, Green Bay Packers star receiver Boyd Dowler separated his shoulder while attempting to block Kansas City safety Johnny Robinson. Dowler's block attempt turned out to be one of the biggest plays in the game, as the Packers' replacement, veteran receiver Max McGee, had a career game. McGee hauled in seven passes for 137 yards, including the first touchdown in Super Bowl history and an insurance touchdown in the third quarter. Before the world championship, McGee had caught only four passes all season while backing up Dowler.

4. FRED WILLIAMSON

Defensive back Fred "The Hammer" Williamson did a lot of talking prior to Super Bowl I. Mostly he talked about taking out the Green Bay receivers, but in the end, Williamson was the one to be taken out. Late in the game, with his Chiefs hopelessly behind, Williamson charged from his corner spot to defend a sweep play. He dived for Green Bay running back Donny Anderson, but Anderson's knee met the Hammer's head and Williamson suffered a concussion. To add insult to injury, the defensive back had to be carried off the field. To add injury to insult, he also had his arm broken when a teammate fell on him while he lay on the grass after the play.

5. JACK YOUNGBLOOD

During his career with the Los Angeles Rams, Jack Youngblood was considered a warrior at his defensive end spot, playing in 245 consecutive games. He proved his grit in the 1979 postseason, with a courageous performance for the ages. The Rams had a reputation as a bridesmaid in the NFC playoffs. In the ten years prior to '79, the Rams were fixtures in the playoffs but were shut out of the Super Bowl, as the Vikings went to the big game four times and the Cowboys, five. But in '79, the Rams caught fire, upsetting Dallas at Texas Stadium in the divisional round of the playoffs. During that game, Youngblood broke his left leg. Despite the protests of the medical staff, Youngblood returned to the field to play in the Rams' win over Tampa Bay in the NFC Championship Game, and then he played the entire Super Bowl XIV loss to the Steelers.

6. TERRY BRADSHAW

In Super Bowl X quarterback Terry Bradshaw was knocked out of the game on perhaps his finest throw, a 64-yard touchdown pass to receiver Lynn Swann with 3:02 remaining. Cowboys defensive end Larry Cole and safety Cliff Harris nailed Bradshaw on the play. The score gave Pittsburgh a 21–10 lead over Dallas, but when Dallas scored a quick touchdown, backup quarterback Terry Hanratty ran four straight running plays for the Steelers, turning it over to the Cowboys one last time. Dallas's effort fell short, but those last few minutes showed how vulnerable the Steelers were with Bradshaw on the sidelines.

7. TERRELL DAVIS

Broncos star running back Terrell Davis left Super Bowl XXXII in the second quarter with his team on top of the Green Bay Packers. Davis stayed in the locker room with a painful migraine until the third quarter began. It was a tense wait through halftime for Broncos fans, but whatever he took, it worked, because Davis rushed for more than 90 yards and two of his three touchdowns in the second half as Denver upset Green Bay.

8. TROY AIKMAN

In their 1993 NFC Championship Game win over the 49ers, Cowboys quarterback Troy Aikman suffered a concussion that knocked him out of the game. Although Aikman's concussion did not appear serious at the time, Bernie Kosar came in to finish the game and even threw an important touchdown pass. Aikman came back to play with the concussion one week later in Super Bowl XXVIII against the Bills. Despite leading Dallas to their second straight Super Bowl championship, Aikman has long maintained that the concussion affected him so much that he does not remember much of his second big game win.

Jon SooHoo

Troy Aikman shook off the effects of a concussion to lead the
Cowboys to a 30–13 win over the Bills in Super Bowl XXVIII.

9. DREW BLEDSOE

The Patriots were on their way to a 0–2 start to the 2001 season. Late in the fourth quarter, quarterback Drew Bledsoe received a vicious hit from Jets linebacker Mo Lewis that sidelined him for many weeks. In stepped little-known backup Tom Brady, who just a year earlier had been New England's *fourth* string quarterback. The rest, as they say, is history. Brady has gone 41–12 as a starter and led the Patriots to championships in Super Bowls XXXVI and XXXVIII. Bledsoe was traded in the off-season to division rival Buffalo.

10. BOB GRIESE

Bob Griese was the Dolphins' starting quarterback for their three consecutive Super Bowl appearances in the early 1970s, but in 1972 Griese broke his right leg in the fifth game of the season against San Diego. The Dolphins continued their perfect season with backup Earl Morrall at the helm, but Morrall struggled somewhat in the AFC Championship Game in Pittsburgh, and Griese came on to finish off a 21–17 victory. Despite not starting a game since October, Griese was inserted into the lineup for Super Bowl VII, and in the big game he helped finish off a perfect 17–0 record with a 14–7 win over the Redskins.

Fond Farewells

"Parting is such sweet sorrow." Perhaps there is no better reflection of Shakespeare's sentiment than football players who finish their career with the Super Bowl. Great coaches and great players have all said their goodbyes, in victory and defeat, at the big game.

1. VINCE LOMBARDI

Coach Vince Lombardi is the most famous person to call it quits following the Super Bowl. He announced his retirement from the Packers following their Super Bowl II win over the Raiders. In his nine years in Wisconsin, his teams won five world championships and two Super Bowls. Lombardi did come out of retirement two seasons later to lead the Washington Redskins, but Super Bowl II was his last game with the team for which he will be permanently linked.

2. JOHN ELWAY

The knock on quarterback John Elway for fifteen seasons was that he couldn't win the big one. His Broncos had been embarrassed in three Super Bowls, and despite his remarkable talent and his team's fabulous record, his Super Bowl games cast a huge shadow on his career. That all changed with Denver's win in Super Bowl XXXII over the Packers. There was some question as to whether Elway would return to the team for the 1998 season or opt for retirement. But Elway returned, culminating a two-year championship run by winning the MVP in Denver's Super Bowl XXXIII win over Atlanta.

3. MATT MILLEN

In a twelve-year career with three franchises, linebacker Matt Millen was part of four Super Bowl championship teams. He won the Super Bowl as a rookie with Oakland in 1980, won again with the Raiders in 1983, then triumphed with San Francisco in Super Bowl XXIV, and was on the Redskins' roster for their Super Bowl XXVI win over the Bills, although he did not play. Playing with the 1991 champs was Millen's last hurrah on the field before moving up to the broadcast booth and eventually to the Detroit Lions' front office.

4. BILL WALSH

The king of the West Coast offense and architect of the 49ers' dynasty of the 1980s, head coach Bill Walsh called it quits following San Francisco's win over Cincinnati in Super Bowl XXIII. That win was Walsh's third, and the third of five the 49ers have claimed. This last Walsh triumph was emotional for the head coach in a number of ways: His team made a dramatic comeback to pull out a 20–16 win; Cinncinati's coach, Sam Wyche, was an assistant on Walsh's first Super Bowl winner; and finally, he led San Francisco with the knowledge that this was, in fact, his final game. Just a couple of days later, Walsh announced his retirement. Although he did go on to coach at Stanford and later moved back to the 49ers' front office, he never returned to an NFL sideline.

5. JACKIE SMITH

Raise your hand if you knew that tight end Jackie Smith, perhaps best known for dropping a sure touchdown pass in Super Bowl XIII, is in the Hall of Fame. Smith played fifteen years for the St. Louis Cardinals before being talked into playing one more year for the Cowboys in 1978. He had never won a Super Bowl (or a playoff game for that matter) with the Cardinals, so he joined the Cowboys for a last shot at glory. His Super Bowl XIII drop turned out to be his final act as a pro, as he retired after the game. One interesting piece of trivia about that Smith drop: During the 1978 regular season, Smith had zero receptions.

6, 7, 8. TOM JACKSON, LOUIS WRIGHT, STEVE FOLEY

Tom Jackson, Louis Wright, and Steve Foley were anchors for the Broncos' defense for a decade. All three started for Denver in Super Bowl XII against Dallas, and all three were still there when the Broncos made their return to the big game nine years later. Super Bowl XXI against the Giants marked the end of the careers of all three. Jackson was with the Broncos the longest as an outside linebacker who spent fourteen years in Mile High, recorded twenty interceptions, and went to three Pro Bowls. Wright, a starter at cornerback, went to five Pro Bowls in his twelve-year career and recorded twenty-six interceptions. Foley started at both cornerback and free safety during his eleven years in Denver and to this day holds the Broncos' career interception record with forty-four.

9. MEL RENFRO

Mel Renfro anchored the secondary of Dallas for fourteen years, from 1964 through the Cowboys' win in Super Bowl XII against the Broncos following the 1977 season. During his Hall of Fame career, he played in four Super Bowls, winning two. He was also involved in one of the stranger plays in Super Bowl history. He tipped a ball in Super Bowl V that Colts tight end John Mackey caught and ran in for a 75-yard touchdown.

10. JIMMY JOHNSON

Jimmy Johnson was the key figure in the Cowboys' resurgence in the early 1990s, and coached Dallas to two world championships in Super Bowls XXVII and XXVIII. But dealing with Dallas owner Jerry Jones became too much for Johnson, and the two reached a mutual termination agreement two months after his last Super Bowl triumph. Although the Cowboys won Super Bowl XXX with Barry Switzer and Johnson went on to coach the Dolphins, neither the team nor the coach ever enjoyed the same success they had in the magical years of 1992 and 1993.

nails in the Coffin

Yogi Berra once said that "it ain't over till it's over," but sometimes the Super Bowl is over before the final gun. Many times fans can point to one moment when the big game, for all intents and purposes, has ended.

1. WILLIE WOOD

With his Packers leading the upstart Chiefs 14–10 early in the third quarter of Super Bowl I, veteran cornerback Willie Wood put the hammer to Kansas City. Chiefs quarterback Lenny Dawson, under a heavy rush, tossed an ill-advised pass into the left flat. Wood picked it off in stride at midfield and returned the ball 45 yards to the Kansas City 5-yard line. One play later the Packers led 21–10 on Elijah Pitts's touchdown run. Kansas City did not challenge again as the Packers won, 35–10.

2. LYNN SWANN

With just three minutes left in Super Bowl X, Pittsburgh quarterback Terry Bradshaw was knocked out of the game on a vicious hit delivered on a pass attempt for receiver Lynn Swann. But Swann delivered the knockout blow to the Cowboys, scooting into the end zone for a 64-yard touchdown that gave the Steelers a 21–10 lead.

3.   JOHN RIGGINS

Despite outplaying the Dolphins throughout Super Bowl XVII, the Redskins found themselves trailing 17–13 in the fourth quarter, thanks to two long Miami touchdowns. That's when Redskins running back John Riggins took over. On a fourth-and-one play, he rumbled for 43 of his 166 yards and a touchdown to give Washington a lead they never relinquished.

4.   WILLIE BROWN

The Raiders were well on their way to winning Super Bowl XI, when cornerback Willie Brown put the Vikings out of their misery early in the fourth quarter. Minnesota quarterback Fran Tarkenton tried to rally his team from a big deficit, but his pass toward the left sideline was intercepted by the old-timer Brown, who coasted untouched for 75 yards and the touchdown that gave the Raiders a 32–7 lead and their first Super Bowl championship. The NFL Films footage of Brown, a close-up on his face as he chugs toward the end zone, is one of their most famous clips.

5.   JOE MONTANA AND JERRY RICE

The 49ers hit the Denver Broncos early and often in Super Bowl XXIV, but it was late in the second quarter when two Hall of Famers delivered the knockout blow. Leading 20–3 with thirty-four seconds remaining in the half, quarterback Joe Montana hooked up with receiver Jerry Rice on a 38-yard touchdown to make the score 27–3. With a 24-point lead, San Francisco didn't break a sweat for the rest of the game as they won their fourth Super Bowl championship.

6.   TROY AIKMAN AND MICHAEL IRVIN

The Buffalo Bills kept Super Bowl XXVII close for most of the first half, but just before halftime, quarterback Troy Aikman and receiver Michael Irvin took over for Dallas. With less than two minutes to go before intermission, Aikman connected with Irvin on a 19-yard touchdown pass to give Dallas a 21–10 lead. Just eighteen seconds later, following a Thurman Thomas fumble, the two hooked up again on an 18-yard touchdown. That second score gave the Cowboys an eighteen-point lead (that's a lot of eighteens, if you're scoring at home) and the 52–17 rout was on.

7.   LARRY BROWN

Super Bowl XXX had tightened up. Once trailing the Cowboys by thirteen points, the Steelers had trimmed Dallas's lead to just 20–17 with a little less than ten minutes to play. But Dallas cornerback Larry Brown drove a stake into Pittsburgh's heart when he cradled an errant Neil O'Donnell pass and returned it inside the Steelers' 10-yard line. Shortly thereafter, running back Emmitt Smith scored to give the Cowboys their 27–17 winning margin. Brown's interception was his second in the second half; both had set up Dallas scores.

8.   ROD SMITH

Super Bowl XXXIII looked like it had the chance to be a competitive game. With a little over five minutes left in the second quarter, Atlanta's Morten Andersen lined up for a short field goal attempt that, if successful, would pull the Falcons to within 10–6 of the Denver Broncos. But Andersen, who had hit the overtime field goal in Minnesota to send the Falcons to the Super Bowl, missed the kick, and on the next play, Denver wide receiver Rod Smith hauled in an 80-yard touchdown pass behind safety Eugene Robinson to give the Broncos a two-touchdown lead. The Falcons never were able to make a game of it after that play.

9. DESMOND HOWARD

The momentum seesawed in Super Bowl XXXI. The Green Bay Packers jumped out to a 10-0 lead but then fell behind the New England Patriots, 14–10. Then the Packers came back with seventeen straight points to give them a 27–14 lead, before a third-quarter touchdown brought New England within six points. On Adam Vinatieri's ensuing kickoff, Packers wide receiver Desmond Howard raced 99 yards unimpeded for a touchdown that sealed Green Bay's first Super Bowl win since Super Bowl II.

10. DWIGHT SMITH

Tampa Bay was on their way to overwhelming the Oakland Raiders in Super Bowl XXXVII when Buccaneers defensive back Dwight Smith put the hammer down on the Silver and Black. Tampa Bay had just scored a touchdown in the third quarter to go up 27–3, but with the Raiders' high-octane offense, a comeback was not out of the question. But when Dwight Smith stepped in front of Raiders receiver Jerry Rice on an out pattern to the left sideline and raced 44 yards for the touchdown, he erased all doubt of the outcome.

A Lott of Big Wins

The San Francisco 49ers owned the decade of the eighties, winning four Super Bowls in a nine-year span. All of this was quite surprising considering their record in 1979 was 2–14 and they were only a slightly better 6–10 the following year. But everything came together in 1981, and they capped their decade at the top with a near-flawless performance in Super Bowl XXIV following the 1989 season.

1. THE CATCH THAT STARTED IT ALL

San Francisco played host to the Dallas Cowboys in the 1981 NFC Championship Game, and even though the upstart 49ers had defeated the Cowboys 45–14 during the regular season, most observers expected the veteran Cowboys to advance to their sixth Super Bowl. In a game that seesawed back and forth, Dallas scored ten fourth-quarter points to grab a 27–21 lead and looked like they were in control, but with less than five minutes to play, Joe Montana led the 49ers on a drive from their own 10-yard line deep into Dallas territory. With the ball on the 6 and facing third down, Montana rolled to his right and was chased by three Cowboys. Nearing the sideline, he chucked the ball up toward the back of the end zone. At first look, it seemed he was throwing the ball away to avoid a loss of yardage, but from out of nowhere, wide receiver Dwight Clark made a leaping fingertip catch over the Cowboys' Everson Walls to give San Francisco a 28–27 lead with fifty-one seconds left on the clock. "The Catch," as Clark's play came to be known, launched the 49ers into Super Bowl XVI and is widely regarded as the official starting-off point of the San Francisco dynasty.

2.   RUNNING GAME? WHO NEEDS A RUNNING GAME?

An old saying in the NFL goes: If you want to win, you need to be able to run the ball, and you need to stop the run. But the 49ers' offense in Super Bowl XVI proved that that's not always the case. Their leading rusher in 1981 was Ricky Patton, who had 533 yards on the ground. Their other running backs were Earl Cooper, Bill Ring, Johnny Davis, and Amos Lawrence. If you're scratching your head right now and thinking "Who?" you're not alone; none of those guys will make anyone forget the Steelers' Franco Harris or the Bears' Walter Payton. The San Francisco West Coast offense was not predicated on a strong running game, so a marquee back was unnecessary. The 49ers did upgrade the position for their next trip to the Super Bowl, however. For Super Bowl XIX they had both Roger Craig and Wendell Tyler on the roster.

3. **THE GOAL-LINE STAND**

Three plays from the 1-yard line defined the defense of
the 49ers in Super Bowl XVI. Leading the Bengals
20–7 late in the third quarter and momentum threaten-
ing to swing back Cincinnati's way, the 49ers pulled off
the greatest goal-line stand in Super Bowl history. On
first down from the 3-yard line, Bengals bruising back
Pete Johnson bulled his way to the 1. On second down
Johnson got the call again but was stopped by a con-
voy led by Hacksaw Reynolds. On third down quarterback Ken Anderson opted for a play action pass, and
the call worked. He hit running back Charles
Alexander out of the backfield off right end, but
Alexander cut his route short of the goal line, and
49ers linebacker Dan Bunz made an incredible open-
field tackle to stop him shy of the end zone. Then on
fourth down, Johnson was again stopped by Reynolds
and crew, despite San Francisco having the wrong per-
sonnel and only ten men on the field.

4. **NEAR PERFECTION**

For all the talk about the 1985 Chicago Bears and their
quest for a perfect season, many forget that the 49ers
of 1984 almost pulled off the perfect feat themselves.
They stumbled once, to a weak Pittsburgh Steelers
team in week seven at Candlestick Park. The final
score was 20–17. Considering that they went on to win
the Super Bowl, they were only a single field goal away
from a potential 19–0 record.

5. **SHUTTING DOWN MARINO**

The big media story in the week leading up to Super
Bowl XIX was the potent Miami Dolphins offense, led

by second-year phenom quarterback Dan Marino. Many of the 49ers took umbrage that they were being considered an afterthought, especially since they won fifteen games during the regular season and had a pretty good quarterback of their own, who happened to already have a Super Bowl ring. Once the game started, Marino looked like a second-year player. The 49er defense harassed him all afternoon, and although he completed twenty-nine of fifty passes, he only had one touchdown and was intercepted twice. San Francisco got their second world championship with a 38–16 victory.

6. JOHN CANDY

The 49ers trailed the Bengals by three points late in the fourth quarter of Super Bowl XXIII when San Francisco began a drive at their own 8-yard line. This was the time San Francisco looked to the leadership of Joe Montana, their veteran quarterback who already had been through Super Bowl wars. As the 49ers gathered to huddle during a television time out, the offense expected to hear how they were going to execute this incredibly important drive. Instead, Montana wanted to talk about John Candy. He told his teammates to check out the crowd because he saw the actor known for his role in *Planes, Trains, and Automobiles* sitting up in the stands. Montana's quips brought a little levity to the huddle and loosened up the 49ers enough to march down the field for the winning score.

7. POURING IT ON

Super Bowl XXIV was a loud exclamation point on the decade of the 49ers. With the Denver Broncos standing in their way, San Francisco attempted to become the second franchise to ever win four Super Bowls. Joe Montana, Jerry Rice, and the gang were just not going to let Denver stop them, running up 461 yards of offense and eight touchdowns (two in each quarter). They set a record for points scored in a single Super Bowl game with fifty-five, and they probably could have scored more.

8. THE FIVE WITH FOUR

Only five men were with the 49ers for all four of their Super Bowl wins in the eighties. Joe Montana was one of two on the offensive side of the ball. The other? Reserve wide receiver Mike Wilson. On the defensive side, both Eric Wright and Ronnie Lott were rookies for Super Bowl XVI and played on all four Super Bowl winners with linebacker Keena Turner.

9. AN UNSTOPPABLE CHARGE

Super Bowl XXIX marked the first time in six seasons that the 49ers returned to the big game. Jerry Rice was still around, but a new quarterback was in charge: Steve Young, who for all his magical talent, was much maligned because he did not have the four rings that his predecessor, Joe Montana, did. Young took his frustrations out on the San Diego Chargers, tossing a Super Bowl–record six touchdown passes in a 49–26 demolition.

10. GEORGE SEIFERT

Not many men who coach two Super Bowl champions are considered an afterthought, and for the most part, George Seifert is remembered as the guy who replaced Bill Walsh. Seifert ought to be remembered

Jon SooHoo

Steve Young finally earned a Super Bowl ring with his MVP performance in the 49ers' Super Bowl XXIX win over the Chargers.

for his tremendous regular season winning percentage (at least during his tenure with San Francisco and not later with Carolina) and the fact that he was at the helm for two of the biggest blowouts in Super Bowl history: Super Bowls XXIV and XXIX. Of the coaches who've won two Super Bowl titles, only the Raiders' Tom Flores gets less respect for his coaching ability.

The Steel Curtain

The Super Bowl era has never seen a more domi-
nant team than Chuck Noll's 1974–79 Pittsburgh
Steelers. In a span of six years, the Steelers won four
Super Bowls and went to the AFC Championship
Game with their two top running backs injured. Terry
Bradshaw is one of only two quarterbacks to win four
Super Bowls, and Noll is the only head coach with four
wins. They had a dominant defense, a power running
game, flashy receivers with a penchant for big plays,
and a will to win unmatched in an era of great teams.

1. THE 1974 DRAFT

The Steelers were a good team before the 1974 draft,
having advanced to the playoffs the previous two seasons, but that year's historic draft provided the final
pieces to their championship puzzle and was arguably
the best for any team in NFL history. With four of their
first five picks, the Steelers chose receiver Lynn
Swann, linebacker Jack Lambert, receiver John
Stallworth, and offensive lineman Mike Webster. Not

bad, huh? Those four played a vital role in all four Super Bowl championships, and all wound up enshrined in the Pro Football Hall of Fame.

2. FRANCO HARRIS

A symbol of the franchise for his catch and run with the Immaculate Reception in the 1972 playoffs versus the Raiders, running back Franco Harris became the Steelers' first Super Bowl MVP when he battered the Vikings in Super Bowl IX. Franco rushed for a then-record 158 yards and the team's very first Super Bowl touchdown. Although his rushing numbers went down considerably in the next three World Championship Games, he is the only Steeler to tally four career Super Bowl touchdowns, including an enormous score in the fourth quarter of Super Bowl XIII to give Pittsburgh a 28–17 lead over Dallas.

3. TERRY BRADSHAW

Known to a new generation of fans as the FOX Sports' pregame show resident funnyman, Terry Bradshaw was the best money quarterback of his generation. Some, like Archie Manning, had stronger arms; some, like Roger Staubach, were more fleet of foot. But when a play had to get made, Bradshaw usually made it. When the Vikings drew within 9–6 in the fourth quarter of Super Bowl IX, Bradshaw led the Steelers on an extended drive for the touchdown that iced the game. With Super Bowl X still in doubt, he hooked up with Lynn Swann on a 64-yard touchdown—despite being knocked out mid-throw—to finish off the Cowboys. Then in Super Bowls XIII and XIV against the Cowboys and Rams, he threw for six touchdowns on his way to back-to-back MVP honors.

4. LYNN SWANN

If you want to talk about big plays in the Super Bowl, look no further than wide receiver Lynn Swann. His four acrobatic grabs in Super Bowl X earned him MVP honors, and three years later against the Cowboys, his 18-yard touchdown in the fourth quarter put a Dallas win out of reach. Not quite as well remembered was his 47-yard touchdown in traffic in the third quarter of Super Bowl XIV that gave the Steelers the lead. In all, he had 364 receiving yards for his Super Bowl career, and he left a lot of broken hearts in Dallas.

5. THE HATED DALLAS COWBOYS

The Steelers had a vicious rivalry with the Oakland Raiders throughout the 1970s. The two teams met five consecutive years in the playoffs and hated each other. But despite their AFC rivalry, the Steelers had room for another hated opponent: America's Team, Tom Landry's Cowboys. The Steelers resented the fact that the Dallas team got all the attention, despite the fact that Pittsburgh had more championships. Philosophically, the rivals were on different ends of the spectrum: The Steelers had a line-up-and-knock-the-snot-out-of-each-other approach, while the Cowboys had their flash. When they met in Super Bowls X and XIII, trash talk flew from both sidelines, and substance won out over style—but not by much. Both games were decided by four points and could have gone either way. So that should have been it for the rivalry, right? Two great teams doing battle twice in the ultimate game. But, no, the rivalry renewed ten years later in a flag football event for charity, of all things. The intensity was enormous; Franco Harris suffered a broken nose at the hands of Cowboys safety Cliff

Harris, linebacker Andy Russell tore an Achilles tendon, and running back Frenchy Fuqua broke his ankle. Oh, and the Cowboys got some measure of revenge with a three-point win.

6. THE STEEL CURTAIN

The Steel Curtain front four—Dwight White, Mean Joe Greene, L. C. Greenwood, and Ernie Holmes—first played together in 1972. It's hardly a coincidence that that was the year the Steelers won their first division championship. They were never better than when shutting down the Vikings in Super Bowl IX, a game in which they held Minnesota to 17 yards on the ground, intercepted a pass (Greene), recovered a fumble (Greene again), and recorded a safety (White).

7. JACK LAMBERT

Linebacker Jack Lambert was the meanest looking human you'd ever want to see. Remember Richard Kiel, the giant of an actor from the James Bond movies? Lambert looked like his meaner older brother, and he was just as scary to opposing offenses. He personified the toughness of the Steelers' defense best in Super Bowl X, following a Roy Gerela missed field goal. Dallas safety Cliff Harris taunted Pittsburgh's dejected kicker as Gerela cursed himself and made the mistake of letting Lambert see what he was doing. Lambert interceded, grabbed Harris by the shoulder pads, and threw him to the ground. No penalty was called, and a message was sent.

8. JOHN STALLWORTH

Wide receiver John Stallworth was overshadowed for most of his career by teammate Lynn Swann, but he had the better career numbers and eventually made it to the Hall of Fame—a year after Swann, of course. Stallworth had the marquee play of Super Bowl XIV, a 73-yard touchdown catch that gave the Steelers a game-clinching lead over the Rams. The year before, his two first-half touchdown catches helped build a 21–14 lead over the Cowboys.

9. HOLDING OFF THE OILERS

There was a new kid in town in the AFC Central in 1978. The Houston Oilers had brought in Heisman Trophy–winner Earl Campbell out of the University of Texas, and immediately became contenders to the Steelers' throne. In 1978 the Oilers won the AFC wild card spot, took two games on the road, and eventually fell to the Steelers in the AFC Championship Game, 34–5, at a rainy Three Rivers Stadium. The following year the Oilers followed the same path, but the championship game was a bit closer. Houston receiver Mike Renfro caught what appeared to be a tying touchdown pass in the third quarter, but officials ruled that the catch was made out of bounds. Following a field goal, the Steelers scored the game's final ten points and won, 27–13. Neither team made an AFC championship for some time after that game.

10. THE STEELER LEGACY

The legacy of the Steelers dynasty is safe for the foreseeable future. With NFL free-agency rules as they are, it would be impossible to keep a great team together like Pittsburgh did in the 1970s. While the 49ers won four Super Bowls in the 1980s, their championships were spread out over nine seasons and just five players were on all four winning teams.

By contrast, twenty-two Steelers played in all four of their Super Bowls. And while the Cowboys of the early 1990s won three out of four years (something even the Steelers never did), free agency, not to mention owner Jerry Jones's ego, tore the team apart before they could become a long-lasting dynasty.

Hammer, Hacksaw, and Hollywood

Nicknames give an individual a little more personality. And if you've got a cool nickname, then a big event like the Super Bowl is perfect for you—whether you deserve it or not.

1. THE HAMMER

Chiefs defensive back Fred "The Hammer" Williamson got his nickname for his signature hit, a clothesline-like tackle that left receivers loopy. He also hammered opponents with his mouth; before Super Bowl I he boasted that he would take out Green Bay's star receiver Boyd Dowler and bring down Carroll Dale soon after. As luck would have it, the Hammer got hammered and was knocked out of his Super Bowl in the fourth quarter.

2. HACKSAW

Jim "Hacksaw" Reynolds played in three Super Bowls for the Rams and the 49ers and had one of the most appropriate nicknames in the NFL. "Hacksaw" did not describe the way the linebacker cut up opposing running backs; it was a much more literal nickname. During his college days, he took a hacksaw to a car, cutting it in half. That incident only begins to describe Reynolds's intensity. Before Super Bowl XVI, he couldn't wait to get to the Silverdome for San Francisco's game with Cincinnati, so he got fully dressed—helmet, pads, uniform, the whole works—in his hotel room.

3. HOLLYWOOD

You could tell just from watching the opening kickoff of Super Bowl X that Dallas linebacker Thomas "Hollywood" Henderson loved to be on the big stage. Henderson ran 48 yards with a lateral from Preston Pearson for the first big play in the Cowboys' 21–17 loss to the Steelers. Hollywood loved to talk, and that always got him into trouble. Comments he made about Terry Bradshaw in the days leading up to Super Bowl XIII riled up the opposing quarterback, and during a blowout loss to the Redskins, Henderson was caught by television cameras laughing and joking on the sideline, ending his career with the Cowboys.

4. PRIME TIME

Deion Sanders will go down as one of the finest punt returners and cover cornerbacks the game has ever seen. We'll ignore for the moment that he never saw a tackle that he didn't avoid. Sanders got his nickname "Prime Time" during his collegiate days playing for Bobby Bowden at Florida State because whenever the spotlight was on, at the most important part of the game (prime time), Sanders was there for the big play. His knack for delivering at key moments continued through his NFL career in Atlanta, San Francisco, and later, Dallas. Sanders won two Super Bowl crowns in his career, for the 49ers in Super Bowl XXIX and the Cowboys in Super Bowl XXX.

5.   THE STEEL CURTAIN

When you talk about great Super Bowl defenses, the 2000 Ravens are discussed in the same breath as the 1985 Bears. But the standard-bearers of great Super Bowl defense were the Steelers' defenses of the 1970s, winners of four Super Bowls in four chances. Pittsburgh's defense was led by their imposing front four, Mean Joe Greene, L. C. Greenwood, Ernie Holmes, and Dwight White, a unit known as "the Steel Curtain." They were impossible to run on (ask the Vikings in Super Bowl IX), and when opponents tried to throw, they put on a fierce pass rush (ask Cowboys quarterback Roger Staubach).

6.   THE FRIDGE

William Perry did not look like a typical football player. He was officially listed at 308 pounds. Don't laugh now. He was more like 370, with about three-quarters of his weight in his midsection. It was a wonder he ever got his jersey on over both his pads and his stomach. "The Fridge" was an appropriate name for someone who took up so much space, but believe it or not, Perry was a vital cog in the Bears' Super Bowl XX win. In addition to being a defensive tackle, he worked as the heaviest fullback you'll ever see, and for such a big guy, he had remarkably quick feet.

7. THE NO NAME DEFENSE

Another great defense of the 1970s lived in Miami and led the Dolphins to three straight Super Bowls. The first of those games, Super Bowl VI, was a 24–3 loss to the Cowboys and produced a nickname for the Miami defensive squad. When asked about the Dolphins' defense, Dallas coach Tom Landry referred to them as "Nick Buonoconti and a bunch of no names." The name was largely unfair because a few greats played on that defense, including Manny Fernandez, Vern Den Herder, Jake Scott, and Dick Anderson. The Dolphins used this implied lack of respect as a motivating tool that propelled them to two consecutive Super Bowl wins. To this day, though, Buonoconti is the only member of the defensive unit enshrined in the Hall of Fame.

8. HE HATE ME

When Vince McMahon, the CEO of the WWE, decided to launch a new pro football league, the XFL, one of his league's trademarks was the players' choice of what name to print on the back of their jerseys. The XFL player who got the most attention was a running back named Rod Smart, who had the rather dark phrase "He Hate Me" displayed on his jersey. Smart became somewhat of a laughingstock around America, but that did not deter him. A year after the XFL folded, he hooked on with the Carolina Panthers as a special teams player, and one year later, the Panthers were in Super Bowl XXXVIII against the Patriots, with Smart as their kickoff returner. Although he is no longer He Hate Me, the spirit of the name lives on: Panthers quarterback Jake Delhomme bought a racehorse and named the filly She Hate Me.

9. THE KILLER BEES

Killer Bees doesn't sound quite ferocious, but it was an appropriate nickname for the Miami Dolphins' defense of the early 1980s. In Super Bowl XVII they started six players on the defensive side whose last name began with "B." The nickname really stuck in 1984, when nine of their eleven defensive starters in Super Bowl XIX had "B" last names: linemen Doug Betters, Bob Baumhower, and Kim Bokamper; linebackers Bob Brudzinski, Jay Brophy, Mark Brown, and Charles Bowser; and safeties Lyle and Glenn Blackwood. Even three of their reserves fit the nickname: Bud Brown, Bill Barrett, and Charles Benson. All the "Bs" didn't help them in either Super Bowl, though. They lost both games.

10. THE SNAKE

Kenny "The Snake" Stabler had a fifteen-year career with three teams, but he was best known as the gunslinging quarterback for John Madden's Raiders of the 1970s. He was the Raiders' quarterback in the Immaculate Reception game against Pittsburgh; in fact, it was his 30-yard scramble with just less than three minutes left that gave the Raiders the lead in that game. He connected with running back Clarence Davis on a miraculous fourth-down touchdown pass in the divisional playoffs in 1974 to beat Miami and end the Dolphins' quest for a third consecutive Super Bowl championship. He won the double overtime playoff game in Baltimore in 1977 with the famous "ghost to the post" touchdown pass to Dave Casper. But he's best remembered by Raiders faithfuls for being the quarterback who finally took Oakland over the top to win its first Super Bowl championship in Super Bowl XI.

Strange Names, Indeed

If you thought some of the Super Bowl nicknames were weird, check out some of the real names of Super Bowl players. There's no shortage of wacky names in the big games, but here are ten of the best.

1. UWE VON SCHAMANN

Uwe von Schamann had a six-year career with the Miami Dolphins, and during that time he made two Super Bowl appearances as a kicker in Super Bowls XVII and XIX. He's one of five kickers with more than four career Super Bowl field goals, but his scores didn't help the Dolphins all that much, as they lost both games. Von Schamann played college ball on some of Barry Switzer's best Oklahoma University clubs. During his college days, von Schamann had seasons in which he connected on forty-seven and fifty-nine extra points and is second in Oklahoma history with a 58-yard field goal.

2. ALI HAJI-SHEIKH

Ali Haji-Sheikh made his final NFL appearance with the Redskins in Super Bowl XXII, connecting on six extra points as Washington breezed to a 42–10 win over the Broncos. His abbreviated career, over after just five seasons with the Giants, Falcons, and Redskins, was unexpected after his rookie year in New York, when he connected on thirty-five field goals and tallied 127 points, both Giants records. But the former Michigan Wolverine saw his production drop dramatically in the following two seasons, before he latched on with the Redskins.

3. TEDDY BRUSCHI

The first time I heard the name Teddy Bruschi was in the 1996 AFC Championship Game. Bruschi's New England Patriots were hosting the Jacksonville Jaguars, and during the action, NBC's Paul McGuire shouted out, "Brewski!" My initial thought that Paul was a little early for happy hour passed quickly enough, and I realized he was talking about Patriots special teamer Teddy Bruschi who had been drafted in the third round the previous year. Since 1996, Bruschi has worked himself into the defensive lineup and has become one of the vocal leaders of a Patriots team that has won two Super Bowls. Bruschi will go down as one of the all-time great names for a football player.

4. YO MURPHY

When I think of Yo Murphy, I think of an Irish bar sometime around last call, not an NFL punt returner. Yo Murphy was on the roster for the St. Louis Rams in their Super Bowl XXXVI loss to the New England

Patriots. Noted primarily for his work on the punt team, Murphy did have one reception in the game, and it was a big one. He hauled in an 11-yarder on the Rams' final scoring drive and then scooted out of bounds to stop the clock.

5. MANU TUIASOSOPO

Defensive end Manu Tuiasosopo has re-emerged recently, now that his son Marques is a quarterback with the Raiders, but dad Manu was a fierce defensive tackle with the Seahawks and 49ers during his eight-year career. The native of Samoa and later a star at UCLA, his professional highlight came in 1984, when he started Super Bowl XIX for San Francisco in their 38–16 victory over Miami.

6. ZEKE BRATKOWSKI

The backup to Bart Starr in Super Bowls I and II, quarterback Zeke Bratkowski played in the NFL from 1954 until 1971, so he was witness to sweeping changes in the league as a player. Bratkowski also enjoyed a long post-playing career as an assistant coach in the league. I've often wondered who thought the name "Zeke" worked well with "Bratkowski."

7. EARSELL MACKBEE

A cornerback out of Utah State, Earsell Mackbee played five years with the Minnesota Vikings. The enduring image most fans have of Mackbee is from Super Bowl IV, when he injured his shoulder during a tackle attempt against Chiefs receiver Otis Taylor on a short pass play. Taylor broke through the tackle and scampered 46 yards for a touchdown—the final points in Kansas City's 23–7 win. Despite finishing second on the team in interceptions that year, Super Bowl IV was the last NFL game of Mackbee's career.

8.   GARO YEPREMIAN

Poor Garo Yepremian played fourteen years in the NFL and kicked for three Super Bowl teams, but all anybody ever remembers is his flub in Super Bowl VII. Well, here're a few things you may not remember about Garo's career: He started out in Detroit in 1966, and for his career he made 210 field goals and 444 extra points. His best seasons were the three Dolphins AFC championship years, during which he scored 117, 115, and 113 points.

9.   CHRIS HANBURGER

Hold the pickles and relish. Hanburger was a no-nonsense linebacker who fit in perfectly with George Allen's Over the Hill Gang Redskins that went 11–3 in 1972, and advanced to the Super Bowl. Hanburger, at six feet, two inches an undersized linebacker at least by today's standards, always seemed to be around the ball, as evidenced by his six career touchdowns.

10.   RUSS GRIMM

A longtime member of the Washington Redskins' Hogs offensive line, Grimm played in four Super Bowls in his eleven years, winning three of them. How intense was he? Before Super Bowl XVIII, which Washington lost to the Los Angeles Raiders, Grimm was quoted as saying, "I'd run over my mother to win it." Grimm also had an imposing look. He certainly lived up to his name. If you put a black trench coat and a dark hat on Russ Grimm, he'd look like a villain from a Stephen King novel.

Never Made It, May Never Make It Back

After thirty-eight Super Bowls, there are still seven franchises to never play on Super Sunday, one franchise that hasn't been there since moving to its new home, and two who've waited a long time to go back.

1. DETROIT LIONS

They've been playing in the NFL since the 1930s, but the Lions have never made it to the Super Bowl. Since Super Bowl I, they've changed coaches many times, and they've even changed stadiums twice; nothing's gotten them to the big game. The only time they've come remotely close was in 1991, when Barry Sanders led them past the Cowboys in the divisional playoffs. They were blasted in the NFC Championship Game, though, beaten 41–17 by the Redskins.

2. ARIZONA CARDINALS

A franchise that dates back to the twenties, when they were the Chicago Cardinals and played in Comiskey

Park, has never threatened to make their mark in the Super Bowl. In fact, the most noise this team ever made was in the movie *Jerry Maguire*. Since moving to Arizona from St. Louis in 1988, the Cardinals have won one playoff game, their only postseason triumph since 1947.

3. NEW ORLEANS SAINTS

New Orleans has hosted nine Super Bowls, yet the Saints have never come close to crashing the party. An expansion franchise awarded in 1966—the official word came down on November 1, All Saints Day, hence the team name—the Saints have had a number of lean years. They've tried to import big time players including running back Earl Campbell, but those attempts have failed. They've brought in winning, veteran head coaches, including Hank Stram, Bum Phillips, and Mike Ditka, but none of them could turn things around. Even in their good years, the Saints usually end up in playoff disappointment. When they finally made the postseason in 1987, they lost their first game 44–10—at home! The Saints are still looking for their first NFC Championship Game appearance.

4. CLEVELAND BROWNS

Such a storied franchise, the Cleveland Browns have not won a championship in forty years! They've never made the Super Bowl but did play in a number of memorable, sometimes heartbreaking, playoff games. In 1972 they threatened the undefeated season of the Miami Dolphins in the divisional playoff. The Browns led in the fourth quarter before falling, 20–14. Then in

1986, they were the victims of Denver quarterback John Elway's most famous game, when he took the Broncos 98 yards in the final five minutes for a tying touchdown, a play now known as "the Drive." The Browns lost that AFC Championship Game in overtime. The following year Cleveland encountered more heartbreak against their nemeses, the Broncos, as Browns running back Ernest Byner fumbled away a potential tying touchdown with less than a minute left, again in the AFC Championship Game. And two years later the Browns advanced to the AFC championship, only to meet up with the Broncos, again. As they had on the previous two occasions, the Browns went home losers in 1989. Since that game, the Browns have been back to the playoffs twice, and both times have been knocked off by the hated Pittsburgh Steelers.

5. HOUSTON TEXANS (AND BEFORE THEM, THE OILERS)

The city of Houston has been home to two NFL franchises: the Oilers, who called the Astrodome home until they left the city in 1996; and the expansion Texans, who enter their third season in 2004. The Texans have an excuse for Super Bowl futility, being still in their infancy, but the Oilers were another story. They went through a number of lean years in the seventies and then had a great run to two AFC title games under Bum Phillips. The Oilers encountered more success in the late eighties and early nineties with coaches Jerry Glanville and Jack Pardee and quarterback Warren Moon, but the disappointments were many in the playoffs. They endured a crippling loss to the Broncos and John Elway in 1991, and a devastating 41–38 1992 wild-card loss to the Bills, during which they blew a 35–3 third-quarter lead.

6. SEATTLE SEAHAWKS

Since entering the NFL in 1976, the Seattle Seahawks are the only team to have switched conferences twice. They played their inaugural season in the NFC West and switched to the AFC West in 1977. Then in 2002, when NFL expansion brought on realignment, they returned to the NFC West. Not surprisingly then, the Seattle team, seemingly in search of an identity, is also in search of their first Super Bowl appearance. The closest they came to the big game was in 1983, when as a 9–7 wild card, they knocked off Denver and Miami in the playoffs before bowing out in the AFC championship to the Los Angeles Raiders, 30–14. They've since hired two Super Bowl–winning coaches in Tom Flores and Mike Holmgren, to no avail.

7. JACKSONVILLE JAGUARS

The Jaguars began play in 1995, and quickly made playoff noise in just their second season of existence. They upset the Bills in Buffalo and then knocked off the heavily favored Broncos in Mile High Stadium, before facing the Patriots in the AFC Championship Game. They fell 20–6 to New England, but most observers felt the young Jaguars would be back. Following playoff appearances in 1997 and 1998, they finished the 1999 season at 14–2, the best record in the NFL. Both of their losses came at the hands of the Tennessee Titans. And who did they face when they advanced to the AFC title game? You guessed it. The Titans defeated the Jags in Jacksonville, and the team has struggled ever since.

8. INDIANAPOLIS COLTS

The Colts went to two Super Bowls when they played in Baltimore (a home they never should have left). But since moving in the dead of night to Indianapolis in 1984, the Colts have not been back to the big game. They've made the playoffs a few times and played in two AFC title games but can never get over the top. In 1995 they faced the heavily favored Steelers in Pittsburgh and lost when a Hail Mary pass slipped to the turf as the clock expired. Then in 2003 they saw a dream season end in the slop of Gillette Stadium in New England, as the Patriots knocked off the Colts to earn their second Super Bowl trip in three years.

9. KANSAS CITY CHIEFS

The team that represented the AFL in Super Bowl I and won Super Bowl IV has now gone thirty-four seasons without an appearance in the big game. But the Chiefs' dry spell has not been for lack of competitive teams. Kansas City was a fixture in the playoffs in the 1990s under Marty Schottenheimer, and they reached the AFC title game in 1993 behind quarterback Joe Montana but were beaten by the Buffalo Bills. They also suffered bitter disappointments in 1995, 1997, and 2003. In each of those years, the Chiefs finished 8-0 at Arrowhead Stadium and 13–3 overall but proceeded to lose their first home playoff games to Indianapolis, Denver, and Indianapolis again.

10. NEW YORK JETS

The team that made history with their triumph in Super Bowl III has never made it back to the big game.

The Green and White has had its share of lean years, with a notable exception being some of the Walt Michaels–coached teams of the late seventies and early eighties. In 1982 Michaels led the Jets to the AFC title game, where they lost to the Dolphins in the Orange Bowl. After a number of pathetic campaigns, the Jets looked to Bill Parcells to turn the team around in 1997. By 1998 they were AFC East champions, New York's first division title since the 1970 merger! They advanced to the AFC title game, but bowed to the Denver Broncos, 23–10. Parcells is no longer with the team, and while they've been reasonably success-ful under Herman Edwards, they're still a long way from the Super Bowl.

They've Got Personality

There are those who made their mark on Super Bowl history who never made a great catch, never threw a vicious block, and never jarred an opponent with a crunching tackle. Their behind-the-scenes, front-office work, however, was influential in making the game what it is today.

1. PETE ROZELLE

In the 1960s Pete Rozelle was young, ambitious, and innovative, and he changed the face of professional sports as we know it. As the NFL's commissioner, he got owners to buy into his television revenue-sharing plan, and in doing so, he ensured a prosperous league for decades. By pushing for the NFL-AFL merger, he created the sports league to which all other professional leagues aspire. He had a vision that the Super Bowl would become the biggest sports spectacle of them all, even after the poor gate at Super Bowl I (which he helped pull together in a little more than two months).

He believed the World Championship Game could surpass the World Series and the college bowl games, and sure enough, it did.

2. LAMAR HUNT

The young owner of the Kansas City Chiefs and the AFL's primary point person in merger discussions, Lamar Hunt was instrumental in getting the other AFL owners on board with the merger's terms. Negotiations did prove tricky, as most AFL owners were hesitant to agree with anything the NFL proposed. And we can all thank Hunt for coining the term "Super Bowl." Inspiration for the name came to him when he saw his young daughter playing with one of those bouncy super balls.

3. AL DAVIS

Al Davis has long been the closest thing the NFL has had to a cartoon villain. For two decades, the Raiders' executive played Darth Vader to Pete Rozelle's Luke Skywalker. Another of the young crop of innovators who helped push the merger through in the 1960s, Davis worked his way from a college assistant coach to one of the most powerful men in football in less than a decade. But he will always be remembered for his rebellious side and his war with the commissioner. Their animosity dated back to pre-merger days, when Davis, then the AFL commissioner, felt that Rozelle ignored him in merger discussions in favor of Hunt. The war continued for the next twenty years through personal conflicts and lawsuits. Davis didn't always come out on top in litigation, but his Raiders did win three Super Bowl championships, and who can forget

Rozelle's diplomatic congratulations of Davis on each occasion?

4. ART ROONEY

Very few men in NFL history were as universally liked and respected by both players and peers as Pittsburgh Steelers owner Art Rooney. He ran the Steelers for four decades without a single championship to show for it but began to change his team's luck in 1969, when he hired Chuck Noll as head coach. In 1970 the Steelers drafted quarterback Terry Bradshaw with their first pick. And two years later, the Immaculate Reception put the team in its first AFC Championship Game. It all came together in 1974, when the Steelers finally reached the summit, beating the Vikings, 16–6, in Super Bowl IX. There were few dry eyes in the locker room as Pete Rozelle handed the Vince Lombardi Trophy to Mr. Rooney. The Steelers' owner was so beloved that when Terry Bradshaw spoke upon being inducted into the Pro Football Hall of Fame, he choked up when remembering all that Art Rooney meant to him.

5. JERRY JONES

Jerry Jones bought the Dallas Cowboys in 1989 with the team in a four-year playoff drought, and he immediately became known for his slick, often abrasive personality. After pushing out Tom Landry (the only coach in the franchise's history) and front-office executive Tex Schramm, Jones brought in Jimmy Johnson from the University of Miami to guide the Cowboys to the promised land. Jones was not content to sit up in his owner's box smiling for the television cameras. He liked to be closer to the action, often mingling with players and coaches on the sideline. His players loved him because they were well paid and had the best facilities. Once the team started to succeed, Jones and Johnson began to clash over who deserved credit for Cowboys' wins in Super Bowls XXVII and XXVIII, and following the second of those two championships, Johnson walked away. Jones won another Super Bowl in 1995 with his handpicked successor, Barry Switzer, as coach, but the owner's teams were never better than when he had Johnson on the sideline.

6. HANK STRAM

NFL Films can thank a lot of its enormous popularity to Coach Hank Stram, who agreed to be miked for their film of Super Bowl IV. In their 23–7 win over the Vikings, Stram's Chiefs put on a sixty-minute virtuoso performance, but the coach's work on the sideline may have been even more memorable. From getting his team pumped up ("Lenny, they can't stop the short pass." "65 toss power trap, watch 65 toss power trap . . . Hey! 65 toss power trap!") to getting on the officials to laughing at the hapless Vikings' secondary, Stram gave viewers a unique perspective of life on an NFL sideline.

7. SKIPPER MCNALLY

Skipper McNally was a guy who liked a good party, so much so that he would sneak in uninvited, no matter the occasion. McNally, generally known as a harmless fellow, had an uncanny ability to get into NFL parties and the Super Bowl without a ticket. His performance at Super Bowl IV in New Orleans may have been his finest. It's believed that McNally put on a Vikings' jacket, waited outside Tulane Stadium, and when the Vikings' team bus pulled up, he started directing the bus in and walked into the stadium with the team. Undetected, McNally spent the game on the sideline. When it was apparent that the Chiefs were going to win, McNally put on a Chiefs' jacket and wandered over to the Kansas City sideline. When the final gun sounded, who was there to carry Coach Hank Stram off the field? Yup, you guessed it. Skipper McNally.

8. **DION RICH**

Another notorious gatecrasher, Dion Rich claims to have attended more than thirty Super Bowls without a ticket. He's been photographed at many other events, including the Oscars, and claims to have never been invited. Of his thirty-plus trips to the Super Bowl, two stand out: in Super Bowl I, as Pete Rozelle presented the trophy to Vince Lombardi, who stood on the podium next to Vince? Dion Rich. And following their Super Bowl XII win over the Broncos, who helped hoist winning coach Tom Landry on his shoulders? That's right, Dion Rich.

9. **BILL WALSH**

For all his coaching acumen, Bill Walsh could also be known for his sense of humor. Worried that his team might be tight before Super Bowl XVI, San Francisco's first, Walsh pulled a fast one on the 49ers. When the team bus pulled up to the hotel, the players were greeted by a rather familiar looking bellhop. Walsh had donned a uniform and held out his hand for tips. The levity must have worked, as his team looked loose in their 26–21 win over the Bengals.

10. ART MODELL

Cleveland fans may not like to see Art Modell here, but like Pete Rozelle and Art Rooney, he was instrumental in making the league what it is today. When Modell moved the beloved Browns from Cleveland to Baltimore, he was vilified, but just five years later, his new franchise, the Ravens, won Super Bowl XXXV behind linebacker Ray Lewis. It was an emotional scene in the locker room, as Modell, his eyes welled up with tears, thanked his team, and it was a little sad to see Modell win his first Super Bowl after so much professional turmoil.

Bibliography

THE FOLLOWING WEB SITES WERE INDISPENSABLE IN MY RESEARCH FOR THIS BOOK:

espn.com
www.nfl.com
www.superbowl.com
www.supernfl.com
www.usatoday.com

PERIODICALS

Daily News
New York Post
New York Times
Sports Illustrated
USA Today

BOOKS

Baxter, Russell S. and John Hassan, eds. *ESPN The Ultimate Pro Football Guide*. New York: ESPN Books/Hyperion, 1998.

Brown, Jerry, and Michael Morrison, eds. *2002 ESPN Information Please Sports Almanac*. New York: ESPN Books/Hyperion, 2002.

Bouchette, Ed. *The Pittsburgh Steelers*. New York: St. Martin's Griffin, 1994.

Didinger, Ray, et. al. *The Super Bowl*. New York: Simon & Schuster, 1990.

Eskenazi, Gerald. *Gang Green: An Irreverent Look Behind the Scenes at Thirty-Eight (Well, Thirty-Seven) Seasons of New York Jets Football Futility*. New York: Simon & Schuster, 1998.

Fulks, Matt, ed. *Super Bowl Sunday: The Day America Stops*. Lenexa, Kans.: Addax Publishing Group, Inc., 2000.

Kanner, Bernice. *The Super Bowl of Advertising*. Princeton, N.J.: Bloomberg Press, 2003.

Lichtenstein, Michael. *The New York Giants Trivia Book, Revised and Updated*. New York: St. Martin's Griffin, 2001.

MacCambridge, Michael, ed. *ESPN SportsCentury*. New York: ESPN Books/Hyperion, 1999.

Matuszak, John (with Steve Delson). *Cruisin' with the Tooz*. New York: Charter Books, 1988.

National Football League. *The NFL's Official Encyclopedic History of Professional Football*. New York: Macmillan & Co., 1973.

National Football League. *The Official NFL 2002 Record & Fact Book*. New York: Workman, 2002.

Neft, David S., Richard M. Cohen, and Rick Korch. *The Sports Encyclopedia Pro Football, 15th Edition, 1972–1996*. New York: St. Martin's Griffin, 1997.

Nelson, Craig. *Bad TV*. New York: Delta Publishing Group, 1995.

Nelson, Karl, and Barry Stanton. *Life on the Line.* Waco, Tex.: WRS Group, 1993.

Sahadi, Lou. *Super Sundays, I–XII.* Chicago: Contemporary Books, 1978.

Weiss, Don (with Chuck Day). *The Making of the Super Bowl.* Chicago: Contemporary Books, 2003.

Index